US HEGEMONY

Reinhard Hildebrandt

US HEGEMONY

Global Ambitions and Decline

Emergence of the Interregional Asian Triangle
and the Relegation of the US as a Hegemonic Power

The Reorientation of Europe

PETER LANG

Frankfurt am Main · Berlin · Bern · Bruxelles · New York · Oxford · Wien

Bibliographic Information published by the Deutsche Nationalbibliothek
The Deutsche Nationalbibliothek lists this publication in the Deutsche Nationalbibliografie; detailed bibliographic data is available in the internet at http://dnb.d-nb.de.

Cover Illustration:
Burkhard Ebert / Copy Take 16 Berlin

ISBN 978-3-631-59731-6
© Peter Lang GmbH
Internationaler Verlag der Wissenschaften
Frankfurt am Main 2009
All rights reserved.

All parts of this publication are protected by copyright. Any utilisation outside the strict limits of the copyright law, without the permission of the publisher, is forbidden and liable to prosecution. This applies in particular to reproductions, translations, microfilming, and storage and processing in electronic retrieval systems.

www.peterlang.de

Contents

1.	***Rapid change and new formation***	11
2.	***A new theoretical approach***	13
2.1.	Introduction	13
2.2.	The difference between empire and hegemony	13
2.3.	A different theoretical approach: Beyond traditional thinking	14
2.3.1.	An analysis of contradictory terms	14
2.3.2.	The East-West conflict: an example of a power struggle in a dual hegemony	16
2.4.	Essentials of a trilateral axis	17
2.4.1.	The difference between geopolitical stability in a dual hegemony and a strategic partnership between two global players	17
2.4.2.	The trilateral axis as a combination of strategic partnerships and normative consequences	18
2.4.3.	The double structure of interplaying global powers, transnational corporations (TNCs) and financial capital	19
3.	***The rise of the USA as a hegemonic power***	21
3.1.	Forty years of an intra-Western triangle involving the USA, Japan and Western Europe and the East-West conflict as the basis of US hegemony	21
3.1.1.	The intra-Western triangle of US-Western Europe-Japan	21
3.1.2.	The East-West conflict as the second pillar of US hegemony	22
3.2.	The emergence of the dual hegemony of the USA and the Soviet Union	24
4.	***Different patterns underlying the global interaction of powers***	27
4.1.	The USA: empire or hegemony? Two controversial views	27
4.1.1.	The USA as an empire	27
4.1.2.	The USA as a hegemonic power	27
4.1.3.	The USA still a hegemonic power?	29
4.2.	An American attempt to replicate the structure of the former 'East-West' conflict – the tethering of China	30
5.	***The development of a new global interaction of powers resulting from India's emergence as a new global player***	33
5.1.	India's helping hand to the United States	33
5.2.	From non-alignment to an American-Indian strategic partnership	33
5.3.	India's ambitions	35
6.	***The India-China relationship***	37
6.1.	Conflict-ridden geopolitical stability or conflict-avoiding strategic partnership?	37
6.2.	Some agreements called for between India and China	37

6.3.	Implications of India's "realpolitik" with regard to nuclear power, energy supply and its strategic partnership with the USA	38
7.	***India's current course***	**41**
7.1.	The scenario of a new East-West conflict avoided	41
7.2.	India's triangle strategy (India, China, Russia)	43
7.2.1.	India's interregional Asia policy	43
7.2.2.	Russia as a member of the Indo-Chinese strategic partnership	43
7.3.	Agreements necessary for stabilizing the strategic partnerships between India, China and Russia	44
7.4.	Outlook and expansion of the India-China-Russia axis	46
7.4.1.	Outlook	46
8.	***Iran's nuclear policy – A political ball game in US containment strategy?***	**49**
9.	***Contradiction between India's triangle strategy and the USA's assertion of its hegemonic status***	**53**
9.1.	Some discord over the nuclear deal	53
9.2.	The gas pipeline project	56
10.	***Europe's options – factors to be considered by the EU in evolving a suitable approach to the Asian trilateral axis***	**61**
10.1.	Economic interests and geopolitical realities	61
10.2.	Concrete steps in the interest of the various members of the EU	62
11.	***The isolation of the USA***	**67**
11.1.	A flawed perception	67
11.2.	Financial crisis and massive indebtedness	67
11.2.1.	A blow to the self-image of the US-Americans	67
11.2.2.	Some indicators for identifying a crisis	68
11.2.2.1.	More profit from financial investment than from the production of goods	68
11.2.2.2.	Speculation in falling or rising exchange rates of currencies	69
11.2.2.3.	Shareholder attitude and investment in land, houses, commodities and on the financial market	69
11.3.	Some reasons for the US financial crisis	70
11.3.1.	'Failure at a lot of levels'	70
11.3.2.	The overriding aim to globalize US hegemony	71
11.3.3.	The fragile structure of the "global financial architecture" (Geoffrey Underhill)	71
11.3.4.	Simply "New Modes of Behavior" or a veritable "New Deal"?	74
11.4.	Plan B for maintaining US hegemony	75
11.4.1.	"Plan A" – the historical run-up to the present financial crisis	76
11.5.	"Plan B" – Useful results of a controlled breakdown	78

11.5.1.	Crisis management measures for preventing the financial crisis from spinning out of control	78
11.5.2.	The demand for the regulation of the financial markets	78
11.6.	Regulation against the background of varying perceptions of the state	79
11.7.	The state in the hegemonic realm of power	81
11.8.	Conflict lines between the USA and hegemonic formations on the one hand and Continental Europe on the other	82
11.9.	The competitive advantage that the US bailout is intended to achieve	87
12.	***Conclusions***	**89**
12.1.	The transience of empires and hegemonies	89
12.2.	Reasons for the rise and fall of Pax Americana	89
12.2.1.	The phenomenal rise of the USA	89
12.2.2.	Hypertrophic hegemonial consciousness	90
12.2.3.	Rising intra-societal tensions	91
12.2.4.	Indications of US-hegemonc overreach	91
12.2.5.	The financial crisis as a portent for the USA's unavoidable adjustment to the multilateral structure	93
13.	***Afterword***	**95**
13.1.	The present situation of departure – Threat of inflation as the basic problem	95
13.2.	US global strategy as the cause for the present financial crisis	96
13.3.	Closure of the global financial casino as a crisis management strategy for the present financial and economic crisis	97
13.3.1.	Measures for the short-term stabilization of the financial markets	97
13.3.2.	The long-term reform of the economic and financial system	98
13.4.	A historical perspective – Alternative strategies for overcoming global economic crises	100
13.4.1.	The New Deal in the USA	101
13.4.2.	Crisis management through arms build-up in Germany	102
13.5.	Conclusions	102
14.	***Notes and Reference***	**103**
15.	***Bibliography***	**109**

Foreword

After nearly forty years, the East-West conflict ended quickly and peacefully - an end that came unexpectedly for many and was anticipated by just a few. Likewise only a few predicted the financial crisis, which signaled the end of US hegemony. Despite the fact that sufficient information had been freely available particularly in this connection right from an early stage, there were many who acted clueless, uninformed, ignorant or simply remained incredulous right until the very end. For a long time even considerable sections of the political and economic elites refused to look the situation in the eye.

There are many reasons for the growing discrepancy between the possibility of timely realization and the delayed onset of awareness:

- A flood of information converging upon an increasingly hectic pace of life

- A self-sufficing approach in which the willingness to receive information is delinked from the capacity to process it

- The propensity to hold on to theories that have served the preservation of power for a long time

- A fear of the disintegration of traditional hegemonial constellations and an apprehension of the difficulties in constructing new ones

The present book is an attempt to counter such processes of delay. It seeks to enhance awareness of complex development processes and points to ways and means in which global powers could protect their interests without violating the prevailing law, or riding roughshod over smaller powers.

I particularly wish to thank the translator, Madhulika Reddy, who with her persistent queries and numerous suggestions for reformulation, has brought greater clarity to the text.

Reinhard Hildebrandt

Berlin, 2009

1. Rapid change and new formations

The end of the 'East-West' conflict brought hopes of a bright future along with expectations of peace and security. The Europeans in particular were under the notion that the remaining superpower, the USA, would act as an equal among equals and resist any opportunity to build up an empire or a hegemonic structure. But contrary to this illusionary notion, successive American governments perceived the 'Cold War' with the Soviet Union as a real war from which they had emerged winners who - so they presumed - had earned the right to shape the world around the American model of living and American moral standards. This especially came into play after 9/11 when the unconditional war on terror was launched. Inevitably, there was a confrontation between the different concepts determining world-wide interaction among the global players: for instance, leadership understood either as behavior commensurate with an established and undisputed empire or only as characteristic of a hegemonic power, and the difference between unilateral and multilateral modes of action. Even the specific terms and definitions were debated by the academic community. The following sections shed light on the controversial term 'hegemony' and use a new definition to explain the latest developments in international relations more exhaustively.

With the Indian government pursuing a triangle strategy between India, China and Russia – a strategy that has the potential to change interplay between the global powers – an America/Europe-centered view needs to be directed at the India-China-Russia relationship in particular. Was the European Union responding adequately to a new interregional Asia policy and properly balancing its traditional transatlantic relations against a closer relationship with the strengthening Asian triangle? Could the United States under President Bush still be the powerful "informal hegemon" which the Europeans treat as their most important partner? Did the quest for a balanced cooperative relationship require Europe's participation in a renewed containment policy directed at China and Russia? What did the EU stymie to bring US indebtedness policy and US blocking minority within the International Monetary Fund to an end? Why did the EU not attempt to rein in transnational companies and financial capital in their neo-liberal endeavor to achieve global dominance, considering that until recently the Anglo-American alliance proved to be very reluctant to muster adequate counterforce?

2. A new theoretical approach

2.1. Introduction
Keeping in mind that we do not have direct access to reality, and that we rely on the large number of discourses at hand, hegemony primarily raises the question about the mechanism that makes hegemony feasible before we enter the sphere of real politics and the behavior of states.

Usually, awareness of new aspects in relations between nations and regions leads to an evaluation of existing theories. In scholarly discourse, the new phenomenon results in a new term which will thereafter be included among the already existing set of approaches which may, for instance, encompass the following: collective security, complex interdependence, globalization, global governance, informal hegemony, trans-nationalism, two-world order, terrorism etc. With respect to its applicability to perceivable phenomena, each clear-cut model has to show the limits of its validity and exclude the area beyond these limits as a less defined or even non-defined entity, which is partly or completely to be ignored but which may, nevertheless, have an as yet unknown impact on the validity of the model.

2.2. The difference between empire and hegemony
In the relationship of global powers the model of empire rules out a hegemonic world order and the latter dismisses a global interplay of equal powers. For *Stephen Rosen* an "empire is the rule exercised by one nation over others both to regulate their external behavior and to ensure minimally acceptable forms of internal behavior within the subordinate states" (Rosen, Stephen Peter, 2003", "An Empire, If You Can Keep It", The National Interest 71, Spring: 51-61, p. 51).

Immanuel Wallerstein, in his "world-system theory," states that hegemony "means more than mere leadership but less than outright empire." It is "a state ... able to impose its set of rules on the interstate system, and thereby create temporarily a new political order" (as quoted by Ferguson). Wallerstein belongs to the group of proponents who reject the realist/liberal view of state conflict or cooperation, and instead lay the focus on economic and material aspects. In his opinion, the interplay of world powers operates on the basis of an integrated capitalist system, and states essentially look after the interest of the capital accumulated in their national or regional sphere. In keeping with the norms of unbalanced behavior, the more powerful state displays its plentiful resources and material-based authority before its less potent counterpart in the expectation that the latter will recognize the power asymmetry between them. In line with Hegel's propositions on mastery and servitude, the more powerful state anticipates appropriate service from its counterpart. Consequently, Wallerstein comes to the conclusion that empire ranks higher than hegemony. More precisely, an empire is capable of ignoring any measure of autonomy and resistance from its much weaker counter-forces. An empire can stand on its own, whereas a hegemon has to accept the autonomy of other countries and their regionally oriented policies, though it will fight it, even if the result is unpredictable. For instance, *Michael Mann, Joseph Nye Jr.* presented the analogy of a three-dimensional chessboard offering different options: Militarily, the US could by and large act in a unipolar manner; economically though, it has had to bargain on a basis of equality with Europe, while the third dimension of the chessboard ("soft power") involves power that is widely dispersed. In particular, the Bush administration's unsuccessful attempt to adopt a unilateral policy has shown that the USA is not in the position of an imperial power.

Some authors, further, differentiate between two types of hegemony: informal hegemony and hegemony with roots in formal subjugation. Anglo-American journals of international relations tend to portray US leadership as an informal hegemony. Stein Tønnesson indicated why this distinction is vital. "How important is the distinction between informal hegemony and formal subjugation? It is so essential that, for scholarly purposes, formal dominance should be the defining feature of empire. Hegemony is more flexible, more easy to dismantle without armed conflict. Hegemony is less likely to provoke outright local revolts than a formal system of dominance, and is also less likely to lead to conflict with third parties. A hegemonic form of dominance allows for sharing influence with others,..." (*Stein, Tønnesson*, The Imperial Temptation, Security Dialogue 2004 PRIO, vol. 35(3): 329-343, p. 330).

A hegemonic world order provides no real space for challenging hegemonies. Rivals are either considered regional powers still ruled by the hegemonic state (as with China in the case of informal hegemony) or as excluded entities to be cast aside as "pariahs" and very often labeled arch-enemies or devils incarnate (as in the case of the Soviet Union during the Cold War), or - if they are not of a certain size - as rogue states (Iraq, Iran, Sudan, North Korea, Syria) and sponsors of terrorists. For the most, all unavoidable relations with the challenging hegemony are considered somewhat inappropriate, contrary to accepted practice and requiring no mutual acceptance. For a good number of scholars, at the discourse level, "equidistance" was the most unpopular and inappropriate term for analyzing the relationship between and towards the rival powers: the USA and the Soviet Union. For instance, in the perception of the Bush administration, the USA was forced to engage in a bitter war against the completely immoral world of terrorism (the so-called war on terror), with terrorism sometimes lurking behind the acts of rogue states (the axis of evil) or operating through small groups beyond the parameters of all states.

2.3. A different theoretical approach: beyond traditional thinking

2.3.1. An analysis of contradictory terms

There is, however, also a different approach that transcends the limits of the traditional in that it incorporates the position absolutely contrary to what is represented by the term. As for instance in the term *"glocalization"* in which globalization and localization are melded together. Despite its contradictory nature, this term is very often used as a term that avoids certain points of contention.

Such an inherently different approach restores the validity of Hegel's philosophy. Hegel had already realized that terms also include their opposite meanings. For example, the dualities of tolerance/intolerance and power/powerlessness rank higher than their two incomplete, separated, extreme entities. In Hegelian terminology, tolerance and power have their 'total difference at itself'. In the example tolerance/intolerance, tolerance is associated with intolerance in order to prevent the action from reversing into its opposite. Given the wide variety of well-defined meanings and applications of the term "tolerance", for instance in cases of differing convictions, respect for the unclear conscience of the other, repression, its extreme otherness is always contained in the diametrically opposed term "intolerance". That means the term "intolerance" does not stand excluded in its meaning but, on the contrary, is an essential part of each and every definition and application of the term tolerance. Within the range of potential definitions, the borderline between the two different quantifiable entities of "tolerance" and "intolerance" is rarely fixed at the center but rather changes with the context in which the duality is applied. The most extreme condition is the following: intolerance of intolerant behavior aimed at protecting tolerance. The position of the borderline in this case shifts to the position of the entity 'intolerance'. Depending on the specific context at hand, a measure of either tolerant or intolerant elements generally prevails in the dual term "tolerance/ intolerance".

In the example of dual hegemony, the self-determination of the two involved entities requires free choice. Yet, if the only restriction accepted by both is that imposed by their own will, neither would be able to exercise its freedom of choice because the choice of one hegemonic power affects the free choice of the other, and very often repercussions can be perceived only indirectly. As a result, freedom of choice for both requires power to restrict the freedom of the other. Power is sometimes needed to suppress certain choices completely if, for instance, the survival of both is in question or if one hegemonic power is losing its hegemonic status and this development also challenges the status of the other. Power both restricts and enables freedom of choice at the same time and, therefore, no unequivocal decisions – in favor of freedom or power – are possible here.

With respect to the decision theory this means that structural indecisiveness is one of the preconditions along with two other aspects: freedom of action inevitably depends on structural incompleteness, otherwise each solution would have its structurally predetermined place, and no space would be left for new options. Contextual limitations should also be considered. Due to these three reasons, in the decision-making process of each part of dual hegemony, freedom can only refer to the borderline between freedom restricted by power and freedom enabled by power, with the attempt being made by each side to shift this line in the one or the other direction along the axis of freedom and power. This new approach sounds similar to the well-known balance of power theory but there is an immense difference. In the balance of power theory, two separate entities (the USA and the Soviet Union in the East-West conflict) unconditionally confront each other using a variety of hard and soft powers. They are not concerned about geopolitical stability. Their bitter confrontation aims at the complete demolition of the other. In effect, destroying the weaker entity appears to have no negative consequences for the winner.

2.3.2. The East-West conflict: an example of a power struggle in a dual hegemony

During the 'East-West' conflict, the USA and the Soviet Union were pitted against each other as arch enemies and rivals, while at the same time collaborating to rule Europe jointly. At the time of the 'East-West' conflict, the two superpowers, the USA and the Soviet Union, built up a geopolitical stability *with and against each other,* which inevitably led to structural indecisiveness. Self-determination for the two states required free choice, with each state restricted only by its own will. But with reference to their shared geopolitical stability, both of them were unable to implement their freedom of choice without affecting the free choice of the other. As a result, the United States' freedom of choice required power to restrict the freedom of choice of the Soviet Union and vice versa. After the detonation of the first nuclear device in 1949, the Soviet Union entered the stage of geopolitical stability with the USA. Since then, the two dominant states have been stabilizing their European spheres of influence *against and alongside each other.* Freedom in the decision-making process of both superpowers could only refer to the borderline between power-restricted and power-enabled freedom and the effort to shift this line in the desired direction.

However, as opposed to the concerns they shared as a long-lived dual hegemony and in applying the balance of power theory, both continued to predominantly view themselves as, in the one case, a bastion of liberty (USA) and, in the other, a champion of the working class (Soviet Union), treating each other as devil incarnate and arch rival, each persistently weakening the other by all available military, economic and political means and in this way thoughtlessly shifting the borderline between power-restricted and power-enabled freedom at the expense of the other.

Their permanent interrelationship of action and reaction with all available and acceptable means set in motion a double-sided process of movement and countermovement in which their geopolitical stability constantly assumed different forms (*Karl Polanyi*: The Great Transformation - Politische und ökonomische Ursprünge von Gesellschaften und Wirtschaftssystemen, First Edition 1944, Suhrkamp Taschenbuch Wissenschaft Nr. 260, Frankfurt am Main 1978, *Reinhard Hildebrandt,* Kampf um Weltmacht – Berlin als Brennpunkt des Ost-West-Konflikts, Opladen 1987). Finally, the Soviet Union was confronted with a situation in which its power-enabled freedom had dramatically lost out to power-restricted freedom, and the shifted borderline gave the USA an almost entirely free hand. The Soviet Union lost its sphere of influence in Eastern Europe and subsequently got disintegrated.

But some years later, the USA had to accept that the specific form of hegemony it had built up together with the Soviet Union was fundamental to the continued existence of American hegemony. The USA had to recognize its inability to sustain a global hegemony over a longer period of time. Consequently, the Bush administration attempted to build a new dual hegemony with China as a welcome successor to the former Soviet Union. Contrary to the view that posits that the USA is an 'informal hegemony' and China a regional power, the Bush administration accepted China's economic challenge. But China refused to step into the footsteps of the Soviet Union and suffer the latter's fate in the long run. Obviously, the Chinese leaders did not believe in the ability of American politicians and strategists to differentiate between the requirements of a dual hegemony and a behavior that pursues a balance of power strategy. China responded on the economic front, and avoided challenging the USA militarily. Eventually the Chinese leaders formed a trilateral axis together with India and Russia, thus challenging any US attempt to prolong its cherished status as a hegemonic power.

2.4. Essentials of a trilateral axis

2.4.1. The difference between geopolitical stability in a dual hegemony and strategic partnership between two global players

The vast difference between conflict-ridden geopolitical stability in a dual hegemony and geopolitical stability in a strategic partnership between two global players becomes visible in the steady effort of the latter to hold the borderline between power-restricted and power-enabled freedom in the middle, between both partners. In this case, geopolitical stability loses its conflict-ridden, volatile character. As such, it guarantees peaceful and stable relations between two global powers and develops the basis of their strategic partnership. Both members of a dual hegemony are also well aware of their mutual geopolitical stability. But they are always inclined to adopt strategies and tactics that could weaken the counterpart. However, strategies that ultimately destroy the structure of the dual hegemony are duly excluded. On the other hand, as mentioned earlier, global players behaving like *countervailing powers* are not concerned about geopolitical stability in the least. Their ultimate aim is to win the game and destroy the loser. Without doubt, a fragile, conflict-ridden geopolitical stability between two powers remains in place as long as the bitter struggle between them continues; however, it does not pre-occupy them.

If two unequal poles build an asymmetrical strategic partnership, self-control and restraint are required of the stronger partner and self-confidence of the weaker. Otherwise, their partnership will soon be transformed into a simple

structure of subjugation, in which the stronger partner proclaims leadership while the dominated "partner" demands 'real' co-operation. In keeping with unbalanced behavior, the more powerful of the two states displays - on the basis of its plentiful resources and material - its authority over its less powerful counterpart, in the expectation that the latter is able to recognize the power asymmetry between them. In line with Hegel's propositions on *"mastery and servitude"*, the more powerful state anticipates the service it considers appropriate from its counterpart. In Hegelian thought, dependent consciousness has the "being-for-self" of the master, both *for itself* in the master existing outside it as well as in itself (in the form of the "superego"), and actually achieves it in the service of the master and the "superego". However, according to Hegel, it is fully determined only when the "being-for-self" is also for it itself. For perceiving the independent being as itself, it takes the form of "working consciousness". In the process of the thing taking shape, the self becomes conscious "that it is itself in and for itself, in that it externalizes the form" (Hegel, 1973, p.153f). Accordingly, dependent consciousness is determined in its form as "being-for-self" on four counts:
1. through the "being-for-self" of the master which is outside it and for it;
2. the "being-for-self" in oneself ("superego") which has emerged out of fear of the master and substantializes itself in service;
3. the "being-for-self" that emerges in the course of forming within oneself;
4. the externalized "being-for-self", substantialized in the worked object that is acquired by the master.

2.4.2. *The trilateral axis as a combination of strategic partnerships and normative consequences*

To maintain a balance of power-enabled and power-restricted freedom between two strategic partners requires that each country imposes limits on the free exercise of its power. Both partners must make constant efforts to settle growing conflicts before reaching a point of no return. Strategic partnerships consume a vast amount of time, more so if they involve unequal partners. More often than not, a successful resolution of conflicts between two members of a trilateral axis bothers the third. As a result, the process of mediating conflicts is set in motion again and again. At this point, the three-member strategic partnership supersedes any purely power-oriented policies between the three partners and calls for the development of a normative structure for mediating conflicts. In order to maintain relationships within a trilateral axis, the partners must agree upon principles to renew norms and adjust the normative structure to adapt to new situations.

The whole process will be furthered by efforts to prevent an outside power gaining control over the Asian triangle (for instance, if the USA on its own or together with the European states intervenes and tries to rule or disturb relations between India, China and Russia).

*2.4.3. The double structure of interplaying global powers,
transnational corporations (TNCs) and financial capital*

A new interplay of equal partners will emerge in relations between the global powers if the trilateral axis of India, China and Russia is able to consolidate its special relations, controlled by the members' strategic partnerships and if, in the meantime, the European Union is convinced that it is in its own interest to also become a strategic partner. From this point onwards, the USA would have to give up any hegemonic intent and, instead, integrate itself into a new set of regional powers. Already, Brazil and Japan are poised to emerge as regional powers. The interplay of regional powers would create its own rules similar to the "pentarchy" of the 19th century, but would at the same time also have to accept the new situation of intervening transnational companies (TNCs) and financial capital.

For a while, the USA and the UK saw themselves as the home bases of TNCs and global financial capital, offering them the best conditions by providing low-tax havens and supporting their world-wide business through friendly international institutions and agencies. However, in the last few years, both countries have had to accept that TNCs and agencies of financial capital are on the lookout for a somewhat wider basis, for instance a combination of the USA, the European Union and some other countries which, by and large, tolerate their economic power and competitive conditions. The reason for this new development is the ever-increasing amount of financial capital in the hands of TNCs, traditional pension funds, hedge funds, and the merchant and investment banks located in Wall Street or the City of London, which until recently played a major role in organizing the global flow of financial capital. This vast amount of financial capital looked for lucrative new investments in the USA, the various countries of the European Union and in some industrially emerging Asian countries, but generally undermined the authority of states and consequently also the position of the USA and the United Kingdom which had traditionally backed them.

At present, the persisting credit crunch has weakened nearly all financial agencies; it has also affected the hegemonic position of the USA.

3. The rise of the USA as a hegemonic power

3.1. Forty years of an intra-Western triangle involving the USA, Japan and Western Europe and the East-West conflict as the basis of US hegemony

3.1.1. The intra-Western triangle of USA-West Europe-Japan

The fundamentals of a long-term US foreign policy were set down in the Munroe Doctrine of 3rd December 1823. Under the slogan "America for the Americans", it proclaimed the existence of two political spheres, called for an end to all attempts at colonization in the Western hemisphere (thereby achieving a state of non-colonization) and warned of US intervention in cases where the European colonial powers ignored these political tenets. Once Latin America was geopolitically demarcated as America's backyard, the trade relations of the Central and Latin American states came to gradually be reoriented to the United States. Even before the end of the Second World War, the USA brought the South and Latin American states together for the Inter-American Conference of Chapultepec on 8.3.1945. The Act of Chapultepec contains assurances of mutual support in the event of attacks on any of the signatory countries. With this Pact, which was later followed by the Defense Pact of Rio de Janeiro on 30.8.1947, the USA assured itself – just six months before the adoption of the United Nations Charter on 24.10.1945 in San Francisco – that the American hemisphere would be free of intervention from non-American powers. This move was rooted in the thinking that in coming into force, the Charter – which aimed at creating a world order based on the equality of all states, adherence to treaties, peaceful resolution of conflicts, renunciation of force in international relations as well as self-determination for all peoples - posed the risk of America's backyard drifting away. The USA therefore sought - as far as possible - to minimize this risk.

For the same reason, while assessing the risks emanating from its strategic decisions, the USA also took into consideration its relationship with Great Britain and the latter's lingering influence on the British colonies and the former dominions of the Crown. The fall of the British Empire, already debilitated, was as far as possible to be hastened to occur before the proclamation of the United Nations, so that the risk of Great Britain henceforth insisting on being treated on a par with the USA – a risk associated with the Charter – could be minimized.

With the intention of prematurely sapping the British Empire of its strength, America refused to permit Great Britain to settle the war loans raised in the USA with the surplus earned by the British colonies in their trade with the United States, conducted during the period when the war necessarily brought the colonies' trade relations with the dominant mother country to a close. During the war, the former colonies of Australia, New Zealand and South Africa – which though independent for a long time were economically still strongly oriented to Great Britain – turned to the USA to strengthen their economic ties. In the case of Hong Kong, the USA even called upon Great Britain to completely withdraw from the colony. The USA also took yet another negative step to exclude Great Britain from participating in the further development of atomic bombs and missiles, although Britain had taken the initiative to develop nuclear arms and decided as late as in 1940 to re-locate its research and development facilities to the US, fearing the impact of the war.

Finally, at the Bretton Woods Monetary and Financial Conference (1.7.-23.7.1944), the USA prevailed over John Maynard Keynes, the British representative, to establish the primacy of the US dollar over the pound sterling as the world's primary reserve currency, while at the same time ensuring that the USA could exercise its veto powers in the newly created International Monetary Fund against all decisions that went against its interests. This it could do with the help of the vetoing minority it enjoyed.

Even during the Second World War, the American administration, in all its security-related decisions, followed a policy aimed at weakening the other powers, including the Soviet Union, in order to reduce the risk arising from the principle of equality being applied once the Charter of the United Nations came into force of the Charter of the United Nations. The Americans therefore curtailed their arms supplies to the Soviet Union, putting an end to them altogether once it became clear that the "Red Army" could bring the invading German troops to a halt and finally even force them to retreat. Despite manifold requests from the Soviet side that the American invasion on the Western front be launched earlier, so as to provide relief to the Soviet army in the East, the American generals decided to postpone the invasion until the summer of 1944. As with Imperial Britain, with the Soviet Union too, the USA thus pursued a policy of debilitation to avoid being confronted in UN organs during the post-war period with countries that were truly its equals, both in status and in power.

Thus, having secured its own backyard, cleared the way for military, political and economic access to industrialized Western Europe and Japan following the capitulation of the two remaining Axis powers (Germany and Japan), and having assured itself a pivotal position as a leading military, economic and financial power, the USA hoped to be able to push through its hegemonic interests despite the United Nations' demand for equal treatment for all nations in the future.

3.1.2. The East-West conflict as the second pillar of American hegemony
When Churchill, as representative of a weakened British Empire, and Stalin in his attempt to extend the Soviet sphere of influence sought – in the autumn of 1944 – to divide up the Balkans between them, with Rumania and Bulgaria for the most part falling under the Soviet sphere of influence while Greece was declared to be predominantly British, both sides claiming control over one half of Yugoslavia and Hungary, these powers were acting on the basis of scenarios that accorded them the status of junior partners of the United States at best. This plan to divide up the Balkans unexpectedly demonstrated to the USA that despite all its measures to weaken its rivals, it would have to deal with two other victorious powers in the post-war period, who would not only assert their

autonomy but even make hegemonic claims of their own. In order to achieve its goal, the Soviet army for instance demonstrated its capacity to penetrate into the very heart of Germany, enter the war against Japan just before the end of the World War, occupy Manchuria and station troops in North Korea.

At the end of the Second World War when the USA sought to effectively pursue its hegemonic interests, it had to look for ways and means to further weaken its rivals under the more difficult conditions set down in the UN Charter. In the case of Great Britain and its hegemonic aspirations, the decolonization policy propagated with the United Nations promised to become an effective instrument for sapping the British Empire of its strength. In having the CIA stage the enthronement of the Shah of Persia, thereby ousting the democratically elected President, M. Mossadegh, in 1953, the United States not only stifled democracy in Iran but also shut off access to the Iranian oilfields for the British. In the Suez Canal conflict of 1956, the USA humiliated the British government by refusing to de-nationalize the Canal through military means.

In the case of the Soviet Union, the USA could not expect it to relinquish its hegemonic claim so quickly. Napoleon and Hitler were to learn that, by virtue of its vast land mass, the Soviet Union is a country that does not allow itself to be conquered so easily or occupied permanently. As a result, the Soviet leadership could not be intimidated with the threat of a blistering war. Other measures appeared necessary to get the Soviet Union to give up its hegemonic claim and submit to American supremacy.

Vis-a-vis the Soviet Union, the USA enjoyed a distinct advantage in the period immediately following the war: While the retreating German troops had destroyed all traces of Russian industry and a good proportion of the infrastructure except for the production facilities that had been hastily built up in and beyond the Urals, the USA, far removed from the warfront, could develop its industry to the highest technological standards without threat or hindrance. Further, while advancing into areas that were to later fall under the Soviet occupation zone, the US army was to capture German missile experts (among them Werner von Braun) and all production facilities for the V-2 missiles in the South Harz. On the basis of the information at its disposal, the American military leadership reckoned with a period of at least ten years for the Soviet army to acquire atomic weapons and over twenty years for the Soviets to develop a missile force of their own. Thus in the short to medium term, the monopoly on atomic weapons and the capacity for the immediate deployment of long-range bombers would guarantee the USA a head-start which the Soviet side would be hard put to catch up with. Furthermore, the US could maintain its head-start in the long term through the timely development of long-range missiles. In view of this assured lead, it even seemed meaningful to drastically reduce the size of the US army and use the laid-off soldiers to expand the economic supremacy of the United States.

From the end of the Second World War until mid-1949, the USA had to deal with a Soviet Union which, faced with its economic weakness and lack of appeal, was desperately trying to hold on to its occupied territories in Eastern and Central Europe, even in the face of massive resistance from the population there. This only made it that much more unpopular not only in the region but with people across Europe. The 1948/49 Soviet blockade of the Western sectors of Berlin, which were completely surrounded by the Soviet occupation zone, evoked fear and terror in all Europeans, although the blockade of the transit routes at the same time exposed the Soviet Union's weakness in not being able to effectively prevent either the three Western zones from being merged into the Federal Republic of Germany – a process set in motion by the introduction of a new currency – or the spread of the West DM to the Western sectors of Berlin. The USA also held out the threat of a nuclear retaliatory strike in the event of the air corridors – which were kept open – being blocked.

During the Blockade which lasted over a year, the USA emerged as the protector of the people of the Western sectors of Berlin while also establishing itself almost all over Europe as the protector of freedom against Soviet ambitions of conquest. The end of the Berlin Blockade saw the East-West conflict firmly entrenched in American and European consciousness as the second pillar of American hegemony. With its economic and military superiority, the USA continued to successfully extend its sway over the coastal areas of the Atlantic on the other side of the ocean – this despite the impeding conditions set down in the UN Charter.

This phenomenon may also be observed in the Pacific after the Communist Party seized power in 1949, and China began to lean towards the Soviet Union. In the case of China, the USA reckoned that the risk of defeat would be extremely high if it were to intervene in support of the corrupt and unpopular Chiang Kai-shek regime in order to jointly achieve victory over the Communists. Instead, the US directed its security strategy

- from 1945 to the Pacific coastal region (Japan/Okinawa, Philippines and to the US-controlled Marshall islands with Guam as a base)
- from 1949 to Taiwan (following Chiang Kai-shek's flight)
- from 1953, after the end of the Korean War, to South Korea as well
- from the mid-50s also to South Vietnam
- and, furthermore, from 1965 to Indonesia too, thereby establishing control over the Straits of Malacca, which were important for navigation, and the deep-sea passage between the Indonesian islands of Bali and Lombok).[1]

3.2. Emergence of a dual hegemony between the USA and the Soviet Union

When the Soviets detonated their first atom bomb in 1949, they brought American monopoly on the atom bomb to an end surprisingly early, compelling the USA to reappraise its relations with the Soviet Union. Until then, US military leadership in its strategic game had only to steer clear of the option of occupying Soviet territory. The sheer size of the country served as a deterrent to such a course of action. Now there was a further aspect to be considered: in the event of a conflict, the Soviet military leadership even had the option of throwing an atom bomb on American targets which were not all that very far from the Soviet sphere of influence. No doubt the American heartland (except for Alaska) still lay beyond the reach of Soviet nuclear attacks. However, following the detonation of the first Soviet medium-range missile in 1955, it was just a matter of time before Soviet intercontinental missiles would arm the Soviet leadership with a threat potential of this kind. In 1959 the USA lost the nuclear invincibility it had enjoyed until then and was never to regain this status again. From then on, the USA and the Soviet Union continuously struggled to retain their assured second-strike capacity, and in the race to acquire the most deadly destructive capacity combined with the effort to keep the destruction inflicted by enemy weapons on one's own territory down to the minimum, the USA was always intent on maintaining its dominant position as a result of which it was invariably the first to take the next step.

Once the US lost its monopoly on the atom bomb and, more so, once it lost its nuclear invulnerability, a new strategic situation arose for both hegemony-seeking powers, in which geopolitical stability could be established and preserved exclusively with and, at the same time, in opposition to the other in each case. This actually goes against the self-understanding of every single hegemonic power that demands absolute freedom in choosing its means – a freedom that is only circumscribed by one's own will. However, with regard to the geopolitical stability jointly established by both powers, each of them was equally hindered in converting all conceivable options into real policy. For, in asserting one's own will, the will of the other to assert himself was duly restricted. Consequently, both now needed a corresponding potential for evolving their strength in order to prevent the other in each case from only exercising his own will, while opting from among the possibilities of action open to him. Henceforth, the „freedom" of both hegemonic powers lay in choosing between the options provided by building up their own strength and the options that could be countered by the opposite side and therefore effectively curtailed. Crucial at any rate was evolving one's own strength - whether military, geo-political or economic.

Against this background, the USA signaled to the Soviet Union in 1961 that any measure to halt the stream of refugees from East to West Berlin would be welcome. The survival of East Germany was challenged by the three million refugees who had already left the German Democratic Republic, the exodus having an undesired effect on the architecture of Europe. Few people know that the foreign ministers of the United States, Britain and France met in Paris eight days before the Wall was built. The representatives of the three countries "stimmten in der Auffassung überein, dass der Flüchtlingsstrom die größte unmittelbare Gefahr für den Frieden darstellt'. Jede Lösung des Problems würden die westlichen Regierungen ‚mit Eifer und Dankbarkeit' begrüßen."

("...*concurred in their opinion that the stream of refugees posed the greatest immediate threat to peace. Any solution to the problem would be welcomed by the Western governments 'with enthusiasm and gratitude'*") [Kurt L. Shell, Bedrohung und Bewährung, Westdeutscher Verlag, Berlin 1965, p.36]. In this special case Britain and France pursued the same interests, though both governments had to choose between different goals. At that time a united Germany was less welcome to both than their dependency on the USA.²

The expression 'agree to disagree' (as pronounced in 1971/1972 in the negotiations that settled the Berlin conflict) articulated the consensus between the USA and the Soviet Union and enabled both to address each other's hegemonic concerns in an appropriate manner, resulting in joint control over divided Europe in which the West Europeans enjoyed the American standard of living which was higher than that of the Soviet Union, while the East Europeans had to in addition endure a lack of individual freedom. In this way the USA and the Soviet Union together built up a dual hegemony and guaranteed geopolitical stability.

Yet, neither of the powers believed dual hegemony to be a permanent state of affairs. Despite the commonality of their interest at the time, they acted in accordance with the theory of the equilibrium of forces, in which both sides (as discussed at the outset) perceived themselves as having diametrically opposed identities. In aiming to enfeeble each other through all possible military, economic and political means, both sides proceeded as in a zero-sum game, without concerning themselves with the maintenance of the geopolitical stability crucial to dual hegemony. Shortly before the end of the East-West conflict, the Soviet Union was confronted with a situation where its own scope for action had shrunk to a minimum while the freedom of action open to the USA had peaked.

4. Different patterns underlying the global interaction of powers

4.1. The USA: empire or hegemony? Two controversial views
4.1.1. The USA as an empire

There are two notions relating to the theories of realism/(neo-)liberalism that vie with each other in the discourse on international relations: For a long time, the first of the two perceived the USA as a self-reliant global empire that divided up its surrounding territory into a secure zone and an insecure periphery, was responsible for overseeing the welfare of other nations, and acted as a non-partisan peacemaker in periods of conflict. For instance, a total of 375,000 American troops were stationed in 120 countries across the world. The US had a doctrine of preemption and an economic agenda of its own on the basis of a very large and consumer-oriented national economy, with the US dollar as valid currency for the most important raw materials and goods. George W. Bush's administration had little regard for international laws, as demonstrated by the disrespect shown to the **Geneva Convention** through the maintenance of secret prisons (*Tagesspiegel*, September 7, 2006) and a new interpretation of torture. The USA claimed the right of denying enemy states access to space (signed by Bush on the 31st of August and notified on the 6th of October 2006). How could these examples be seen as anything but the hallmarks of an American empire which laid down internationally valid law and carried it through with its overwhelming power. As Michael Cox declares: …"in terms of function, impact, leverage and projection, the United States has all the principle characteristics of an empire" (Cox, Michael, Empire by Denial? Debating US Power, Security Dialog, Vol. 35(2), p. 230).

"Whereas the British were generally quite open about the fact that they were running an empire, few American politicians today would use the 'e' word as anything other than a term of abuse." (Niall Ferguson, "Hegemony or Empire?", Foreign Affairs, September/October 2003). Bill Clinton's national security adviser, Sandy Berger, pronounced that the US is the "first global Power in history that is not an imperial Power" and Mr. Bush echoed, "America has never been an empire . . . we may be the only great power in history that had the chance and refused" (ibid.). Ferguson concluded, "Americans, in short, don't 'do' empire, they do 'leadership' instead, or, in more academic parlance, 'hegemony,'" but in Ferguson's opinion the term hegemony should mean nothing but empire. Apart from some minor differences, Robert D. Kaplan, Max Boot and Peter Gowan followed the same line of thought.[3]

4.1.2. The USA as a hegemonic power

The second notion supported the converse view of a hegemonically oriented interplay between nations or regions. Within this group the USA influenced virtually every aspect of international relations but was unable to exercise absolute sovereignty over the internal dealings of other nations or regions. For Mi-

chael Mann and Joseph Nye Jr., an American empire had to satisfy at least six conditions guaranteeing its superiority over other nations:
First, the United States had to demonstrate unchallenged military dominance, not only in the instruments available for waging war, but also in its capacity to bring the war to a point of peaceful resolution. In recent years the Bush administration had proved itself a failure both in post-war Iraq and Afghanistan. It was a mistake to attribute to Iraq's dictator Saddam Hussein close connections with bin Laden's Al-Qaida in order to demonstrate a linkage between rogue states and terrorism, even though the CIA knew better (*New York Times*, September 24, 2006, Spy Agencies Say Iraq War Worsens Terror Threat - National Intelligence Estimate "Trends in Global Terrorism: Implications for the United States").[4]

Relying on war lords and cleaning up Southern Afghanistan by military means, which partly has the effect of alienating people and leaving the population without economic support right through, was a mistake which inevitably served to strengthen the Taliban once again (Möllhoff, Christine, "Westen hat in Afghanistan versagt", *Frankfurter Rundschau*, September 14, 2006). In Iraq, American occupation policy saw the country descend into civil war, resulting in a rise in terrorism and a rapprochement between the two enemies Iraq and Iran, almost certainly at the cost of American influence (Pakt im Mittleren Osten: Ahmadinedschad sagt dem Irak Unterstützung zu, T-online, September 12, 2006). On the 2nd of March 2008, an Iranian president visited Iraq for the first time in 30 years. Mahmoud Ahmadinejad assured his host that Iran does not interfere in Iraq's affairs. "Accusations of the kind have their origin in the American failure in Iraq" he was reported to have told a Baghdad newspaper (*Tagesspiegel*, March 2, 2008). And, in fact, the USA did actually arm a militia in the Sunni part of Iraq whose primary task was to fight terrorist groups, though after the withdrawal of the American combat troops at the latest, Sunni and Shia militia would fight for dominance in Iraq while involving the Kurdish areas in the north of Iraq in their struggle for supremacy. Thus, the USA would not be leaving behind a country at peace but one destroyed, in which there is danger of a civil war breaking out between various groups of people armed to the teeth.

In Afghanistan the US army lost its credibility and the Bush administration had to accept the helping hand of other European countries in order to avert a disastrous end. Even the German Bundeswehr, long regarded with contempt for confining its reconstruction work to the northern part of Afghanistan, was asked to send troops into the South where inaccurate bombing raids and Operation Rock Hard military operations by the US army had turned the population for the most part hostile.[5] Officially, US representatives paid tribute to the civil engagement of the European armies but their subsequent pronouncements voiced the perceived significance of combining Europe's civil power with the US army's firepower. For a long time US generals did not realize that to be really successful in the war in Afghanistan, US soldiers had to at least be trained to acquire both these skills.

Secondly, the US had to safeguard its interests on its own soil without unsettling or alienating parts of its population - a condition that was severely impaired after the World Trade Center attacks of September 11, 2001 and resulted in widespread opposition to Bush's policy from the American people.

The third condition was that the US had to gain unhindered access to indispensable raw materials such as oil and gas, an area in which it had failed after numerous attempts in Russia, West and Central Asia. The unsuccessful attempt to gain a foothold in Russia's oil-producing industry was a striking example. Another was the unsuccessful attempt to persuade the Taliban in Afghanistan to accept pipelines on Afghan soil which would be used to pump oil and gas from the Central Asian states to Pakistan and India. The projected pipeline right across the Caspian Sea to pump gas from Kazakhstan and Turkmenistan to Turkey via Azerbaijan and Georgia provides yet another example. This project is still behind schedule and will almost certainly be abandoned, now that Russia, Kazakhstan and Turkmenistan have agreed to build a gas pipeline along the Caspian Sea (*Neue Züricher Zeitung* Online, May 12, 2007).

Fourthly, the US had to have adequate economic safeguards to ensure that its economy maintains its competitive edge over its European and Asian rivals. But in the meantime the US economy "has fallen five places from being leader to rank sixth in the World Economic Forum's 2006 global competitiveness rankings", behind Switzerland, Finland, Sweden, Denmark, Singapore, followed by Japan, Germany, the Netherlands and Britain. (Report on World Economic Forum, in *domain-b.com*, September 26, 2006) and is losing further ground following the impact of the financial crunch on the US economy. While American TNCs (Transnational Corporations) had successfully entrenched their presence across the globe, they largely operated independently of the American political establishment which realized that globalisation is not synonymous with Americanization, and the USA has already lost its top position in what was once the economic triangle of USA, Japan, and Western Europe.

The fifth condition was that the USA must have an effective integrative capacity, the absence of which denied it the clinching support it needed at the United Nations for its Iraq invasion, and which failed to prevent the founding of the International Criminal Court.

Finally, America had to dominate in the areas of culture, civil society, and technology. Arguably, the US had demonstrated its ability to tower over the rest in these spheres; however, its inability to maintain effective supremacy with regard to the other prerequisites for imperialism rendered its dominance in culture, civil society and technology inconsequential.

4.1.3. The USA: Still a hegemonic power?
Keeping the above arguments in mind, it would be reasonable to say that we have not been living in a world of American imperialism but one in which the United States tried to assert itself as a hegemonic power. While it was able to influence virtually every aspect of international relations, it was unable to

exercise absolute sovereignty over the internal dealings of other states. Whereas an empire can stand on its own, the US had to accept the autonomy of other countries and their regionally orientated policies. This sort of hegemony is sometimes euphemistically referred to as "informal or benign hegemony" and signifies dominance by "sharing influence with others" (*Stein, Tønnesson*). C. Raja Mohan has outlined a policy that would be suitable for a benign hegemony. His argument runs as follows: "The threat to U.S. security from the ideology of violent political Islam is not very different from the one once posed by international communism in Asia. This threat was ultimately defeated not by military force, but by manipulating its internal contradictions. A variety of factions in Asia - including nationalist and conservative groups - had reasons of their own to oppose communism. Divisions among the communist powers and the inevitable fragmentation of the international Left helped the United States recover ground in Asia. Similarly, exploiting existing divisions within political Islam, letting regional contradictions unfold, managing regional balances of power, and assisting friendly states to defend shared interests in the Middle East are sensible alternatives to the current, costly U.S. attempts to single-handedly control and direct the evolution of the Middle East ... As its margin for error steadily shrinks amidst a global redistribution of power, and a recognition dawns that the United States cannot play god by resolving every single problem in the world, restraint is bound to emerge as a natural course for U.S. grand strategy." (The American Interest, Volume 3, Number 2, November - December 2007). But whether the USA was fulfilling the requirements of an "informal hegemony" is a question that has already been posed and even partly answered.

4.2. An American attempt to replicate the structure of the former 'East-West' conflict – the tethering of China

As early as in the nineties, the illusionary attempt to replicate the structure of the former 'East-West' conflict proved unsuccessful. The United States had begun to fundamentally re-map and re-strategize its concept of a secure area and periphery with a heavy tilt towards China, while endeavoring to achieve possible geopolitical stability with that country as a new counterweight in the place of the former Soviet Union.
Some years after the end of the 'East-West' conflict, the Chinese leadership found itself having to grapple between acting as a possible counterforce to the USA in a conflict situation that would drain China of its strength, and opening up Chinese markets to investment and imports in order to gain entry into the World Trade Organization (WTO). Opting for the latter, China was up against the potential ramifications of having to contend with the US over the issue of the reunification of Taiwan[6] and with the prospect of Chinese markets being saturated with American goods, besides issues such as credit rating and pension funds. Very soon the USA realized that China did not want to enter into a new

'East-West' conflict in which both countervailing powers tested each other's strength - mainly in military technology and equipment. Instead, the Chinese leaders felt strong enough to compete in economic terms, thus compelling the US to devise a new strategy whereby China had no access to state-of-the-art American and European military equipment but, on the other hand, could flood the American market with Chinese goods on the basis of a fixed exchange rate between the US dollar and the yuan.

Encouraged to cash in on the benefits of the open market, China's trade with America flourished to a point where the flood of Chinese goods severely challenged American industry, reduced its production opportunities, and, consequently, induced the American Congress to block the growing surge of imports from China.[7]

On the other side of the Pacific, the Central Bank of China accumulated an ever-increasing number of American treasury bonds. Selling them all at once would mean flooding the global money market with US dollars, thus resulting in a significant devaluation of the American dollar which would eventually culminate in a global financial crisis.

What actually happened in the last years was that the United States and China were laying the groundwork for geopolitical stability – a situation that however differed from that of the former 'East-West' conflict. China was successful in attempting to give the structural incompleteness a new form. As in the old 'East-West' conflict, both superpowers were anxious to use any option to move the borderline between power-restricted and power-enabled freedom in the direction favored in each case, through a permanent correlation of action and reaction that was for the most part weighed down by economic competition. To the detriment of the US, the prevailing structural indecisiveness came to acquire an economic background rather than a military one.

Once the viewpoint had been duly disproved that capitalism can only take root in a Protestant ethic (Max Weber) and would never grow in the soil prepared by Confucian philosophy, the Bush administration had to accept China's economic challenge and say goodbye to its long-held notion that China was still a regional power, dominated by the 'informal hegemony' of the USA (Blume, Georg, in *Die Zeit*, December 27, 2007).

5. The development of a new global interaction of powers

5.1. India's helping hand to the United States

Growing fears of the critical nature of developments in the American-Chinese relationship led the Bush administration to look at India as a potential, willing partner to counter China's seemingly unshakeable self-confidence. Thus India was courted by the US government and invited to join the American-Japanese duo in tethering China.[8]

Asked about the challenge posed by China to the US, Secretary of State Condoleezza Rice replied *"I really do believe the U.S. - Japan relationship, the U.S. - South Korean relationship, the U.S. - Indian relationship, all are important in creating an environment in which China is more likely to play a positive role than a negative role. These alliances are not against China; they are alliances ... that put China [on] a different path to development than if [it] were simply untethered, simply operating without that strategic context."* (Siddharth Vardarajan, America, India and Outsourcing Imperial Overreach, *The Hindu*, July 13, 2005).

The little more than 100 individuals that make up India's strategic community[9] realized at once that this engagement could give India the opportunity to exert considerable influence - to begin with, in the region of the Indian Ocean and, thereafter, in the South China Sea.

As one of the leaders of the non-aligned bloc, India very early recognized the special form of hegemony that the USA and the Soviet Union established after the Second World War, based on the two factors of ideological enmity and rivalry and a third relating to the divided American-Russian control of Europe and some other parts of the world. Indian strategists also discerned strong efforts on the part of the USA to replicate the structure of the former 'East-West' conflict and shape a conflict-ridden geopolitical stability together with China. Thus, given its own objectives[10] and China's rapid advance as a global player of both economic and political standing, India responded positively to the USA. This will be outlined in greater detail in the following section.

5.2. From non-alignment to an American-Indian strategic partnership

India, sovereign but underdeveloped as compared to the industrialized countries in 1955, emerged as one of the leaders of the non-aligned bloc. India learned to play off the power blocs of the East-West conflict against each other, thereby collecting brownie points and purchasing weapons from both sides. Although India had gathered together as much foreign aid as possible, every Indian government attached great importance to remaining strategically autonomous as a vital sign of an independent sovereign power – unlike some other members of the non-aligned movement who lost their real sovereignty and simply became attached to the one or the other side of the American/Russian hegemonic unit as secure areas or parts of the periphery.

But India's centralized planning system had impaired economic growth and rendered Indian industries uncompetitive on the world market. In 1991, India was reeling from a severe payments deficit, compelling the government to open up the Indian economy to freer trade and even to a larger volume of foreign investment.

Thus at the time when the 'East-West' conflict lost the Soviet Union as one of its pillars due to a gradual decline in its power, and the non-aligned group lost its raison d'être, India was confronted by an international community that was less inclined to support the developing countries through direct assistance or loans. India's strategic community was called upon to look for a new and suitable place for India in the international arena, within the framework set up by the interplay of powers, in a world economy that was becoming increasingly globalized.

Particularly due to its highly skilled labor force, India meanwhile had clearly been on its way to becoming a global player in the world economy. "Every dollar spent in India has a better return than is the case with other emerging markets that have a more favorable environment", the global consultancy firm KPMG (Klynveld, Peat, Marwick und Goerdeler) revealed in its study report 'Manufacturing in India'.[11] Compared to other emerging markets such as China, Brazil and Mexico, India fared well in advancing to become one of the top destinations for Foreign Direct Investment (FDI). On the other hand, some Indian companies had already attained the status of transnational corporations. For instance, the Indian conglomerate Tata was the fifth largest steel company in the world; it invested in European automobile companies and was expected to flood the Indian – and later the global – market with the cheapest car ever to be produced (Lamparter, Dietmar, H./Petersen, Britta, Der tadellose Herr Tata, in *Die Zeit*, January 10, 2008).

It should also be borne in mind that the Indian market held out bright prospects, with more than 1.1 billion potential consumers in the very long run – among them a fast-expanding and well-educated middle class with reasonable purchasing power, numbering 260 million with 30 million added on every year. Given this scenario, capital export for setting up industrial production and services had appeared to be a particularly important task for TNCs. A reputed Siemens manager observed that for some products made in India, the manufacturing costs are two-thirds the costs in Germany.[12]

But alongside other emerging economies, India has also suffered from the effects of the financial crunch in the USA and the economic recession that followed in its wake.

5.3. India's ambitions

Irrespective of what the Chinese leaders actually wish to achieve, India's most terrifying prospect had been – and still is – the loss of its strategic autonomy and containment by China within the geo-strategic confines of South Asia. Any means to forestall such a development is welcome to India. Against this background, the summarized conclusions of a three-part seminar organized by the India International Center (ICC) in conjunction with the Association of Retired Senior IPS Officers (ARSIPSO) opened with the following statement: "India could not remain insulated from developments in South Asia, the Gulf region, Central Asia, South-East Asia and the Indian Ocean. India as an emerging power has no options but to play a significant role in the new emerging world order. Within India itself, misgovernance or lack of governance has an important bearing on national security which needs serious attention."[13]

The Retired Senior IPS Officers proposed that India's most severe threat, the conflict with Pakistan and China, should be addressed by a "correlation of forces" to improve the strategic balance in India's favor, nevertheless keeping in mind that "the inner contradictions within Pakistan would inhibit its proceeding very far with the peace process…"(ibid.).

Their proposals to tackle the myriad problems of internal security (misgovernance and the breakdown or abdication of governance, plebiscitary politics, social unrest as a result of economic growth without distributive justice) encompassed the following measures: freeing the local police administration from the hold of local politicians; greater administrative control over local officials; and firm steps against corruption, communalism and the criminalization of politics. Since the Kashmir issue was seen to contain elements of both internal and external security, the seminar paper suggested more dialogue and trade between both sides of the Line of Control, while reaching the conclusion that "the formula to end the Kashmir problem should be left to evolve over time"(ibid).

Without question, once it has improved[14] its infrastructure, safeguarded its supply of raw materials, strengthened its economy, gradually modernized its military equipment, and reduced its numerous internal conflicts, India would have cleared all hurdles en route to becoming a powerful global player; its traditional sphere of influence would then easily extend beyond South Asia.

6. The India-China relationship

6.1. Conflict-ridden geopolitical stability or conflict-avoiding strategic partnership?

If in the past the Chinese leadership, for instance, responded symmetrically to India's fears of being contained within the geo-strategic confines of South Asia, then this would mean that each power already felt threatened by its counterpole. With tactical balance a constant focus, the strategic communities in both countries would persistently search for improvements to shift the borderline between power-restricted and power-enabled freedom in a direction that is in their own favor.

For a short time, the possibility of an increasingly conflict-ridden **geopolitical stability** between China and India appeared to be a certainty. There were some signs that indicated it could even assume a military form. Both countervailing powers did not hesitate to form partnerships with friends: India with the United States and China with Russia.[15] However, China's strategic community did not perceive India's apprehensions as being of any relevance for their bilateral relationship; in fact it even understood India's ambition to become an acknowledged global player of the kind China already is. The Chinese leadership invited India to enter into a **strategic partnership** involving friendly competition with respect to each other's positions, to expand bilateral trade, strike compromises in their conflicts, and initiate an interregional Asian policy that relegates the other powers (Pakistan included) to the sidelines.

Such thinking was widely prevalent, even on the Indian side of the conflict, with signals accordingly being sent across the border to China. The difference between a conflict-ridden geopolitical stability and a strategic partnership has already been explained and becomes visible in the steady effort to hold the borderline between power-restricted and power-enabled freedom in the middle, between both partners.[16] If two unequal poles build an asymmetrical strategic partnership, self-control and restraint are required of the stronger partner and self-confidence of the weaker.[17]

6.2. Some agreements called for between India and China

But opting for a strategic partnership means there ought to be at least a common understanding between India and China about assuming control of what had once been American strategic positions in the South China Sea, the Pacific, and the Indian Ocean. This should necessarily take place because the United States is already past its prime.

A further area of understanding between the two powers concerns financial capital and the TNCs, whatever their origins may be. TNCs based in and depending on the United States, the EC or Japan (or even of Indian and Chinese origin), tend to play off governments against each other and benefit from their weaknesses. But they are not omnipotent and, up to now, have not achieved the ability to shape laws without the interplay of states. Weak governments can also be influenced by governments competing through their associated TNCs. This indirect influence is often all the more effective so that even states like China and India should be careful about TNC activities. To resist the global management of TNCs means more than just relying on the state's own influence on the national market, however big and powerful that market may be.

For instance, what TNCs sometimes understand by good 'labor regulation', was revealed by the Honda management when it was confronted by workers agitating for their right to form a trade union in front of the Honda factory at Gurgaon (Haryana): "Well, if the workers are going to behave like this, Honda will just close down its factory, or shift it elsewhere and they will get what they deserve." (Seema Mustafa, The Nobodies, in: The Asian Age, 30 July 2005). It should be mentioned "that the state government of Haryana had cooperated with the Honda management to ensure that the trade union was not registered" (ibid). P. Sainath commented on the disruptive incident: "In Haryana, Honda did not even have to come into the picture till things went awfully wrong. The police and administration were there to act on its behalf." (*The Hindu*, July 28, 2005).

If, in the future, the international management of TNCs would be able to divorce itself from individual nations or regional states and would be ever more successful in building state-like institutions which rank higher and work better in their interest, then geopolitical stability will be served by a new hegemonic power composed of these world-wide quasi-state institutions and the various national or regional states. Freedom of decision for both would refer to the borderline and attempt to shift this line either in the direction of quasi-state institutions or the national/regional states. The discourse about the so-called failed states indicates the minimum in terms of state that TNCs demand, and the wide sphere that is managed exclusively by private administration. TNCs do not exclude democracy. The sovereignty of the people is simply assigned a less important place than 'democracy' in the form of competition on the world market.

6.3. Implications of India's "realpolitik" with regard to nuclear power, energy supply and its strategic partnership with the USA

"Those in India who marvel at how Mr. Bush could blithely walk away from 40 years of non-proliferation policy do not understand the tectonic shift that is taking place in the bilateral relationship as a result of increasing fears in US business and strategic circles about China", noted Siddharth Varadarajan (*The Hindu,* July 29, 2005). The same journalist mentioned Ashley Tellis, a former RAND Corporation analyst, who argued in his book 'India as a New Global Power: An Action Agenda for the United States,' (Carnegie Endowment for

International Peace, 2005), that the US should not differentiate between the two nuclear powers, India and China. Indeed, the Bush administration had been extremely astute in dealing with India's pride in being a nuclear power.[18]

There are three reasons why India's strategic community and others considered the possession of atomic weapons the most important element of India's sovereignty: Firstly, the threat of Pakistan's nuclear weapons; secondly, India's continued weakness on the economic front[19] as compared to China's strong economy; and, thirdly, compensation for the loss of India's respected position as the unchallenged leader of the non-aligned countries for more than forty years[20].

To gain broad recognition for India as the new emerging global player, some Indians were obviously willing to pay a high price. The price could be a cap on India's research on the production of atomic weapons. For a long time it was left unclear whether the Bush administration effectively demanded such a price or, on the contrary, speculated on the nuclear race between India and China (and Pakistan too). Such a race would involve increasingly sophisticated atomic weapons entailing high costs and definite advantages for American exports of military technology to India. There was another side effect that would have been welcomed by an economically declining USA: the slowdown of economic growth in India and China and, furthermore, a weakening of both economies.

Closely linked to this scenario was the gas pipeline project scheduled to run from Iran through Pakistan. Here the United States welcomed a delay, and even an abrupt termination of the project, which is certainly expected to foster further economic development in and between the Asian countries but limit the USA's scope to play off the Asian countries against each other.[21]

As a result, India's strategic partnership with the USA cannot be equated with a relationship of mastery and servitude. Firstly, after more than fifty years at the head of the non-alignment group, the Indian strategic community simply did not appear to be used to thinking in terms of mastery and servitude. Secondly, the USA had invited India to form a real strategic partnership. Therefore, the American administration should not have used India's shortage of nuclear energy to display hegemonic behavior. For instance, the Indian journalist K. Venugopal proposed that India's strategic community swallow some of its pride to overcome the nuclear embargo and win the nuclear game. (*The Hindu*, July 22, 2005). Venugopal asked, "Was the US promise of international help, to secure continued supplies of enriched uranium fuel for the US-built Tarapur plant and to ramp up the country's nuclear electricity programme, the tipping point for Dr. Singh?"[22] If there is a steady American-Indian effort to hold the borderline between power-restricted and power-enabled freedom at a point equidistant from both partners, an asymmetrical relationship could be avoided. But there are negative consequences for Chinese-Indian relations too, and these consequences need to be discussed in the following section.

7. India's current course

7.1. The scenario of a new East-West conflict avoided

For a while, India had been pursuing its 'shortcut' to achieving the status of a global player, nudged on by the optimism of some generals and admirals of the Indian armed forces. For instance, Admiral J.G. Nadkarni wrote, ". . . Under the new defense agreement both countries will work towards greater defense cooperation which will include more joint exercises, collaboration on multinational operations, access to US weapons and technology, technology transfers, an expansion of two-way defense trade, expanding collaboration on missile defense, increase in the exchange of intelligence, and a number of other areas relating to cooperation in peacekeeping operations and disaster management." (J.G. Nadkarni, Terms of India-U.S. Endearment, in *The Asian Age*, 30 July, 2005). If India's policy had evolved in line with Nadkarni's ideas, the USA would have taken the place of Russia as India's main supplier of military equipment, a position Russia held for a long time.

At that time an Indian expert on international relations asked himself whether he would like to see the USA or China on the winning side of a new 'East-West' conflict. His answer came as no surprise. Because China is geographically closer to India, his preference was for the United States, even if the Bush administration could be expected to make a failure of it as it did in the Iraq war. If more influential Indian experts were to have responded in similar fashion[23], the interplay of world powers would have shifted in the following direction:

The partnership between India and the United States could be expected to bring China and Russia closer together, with a Chinese-Russian partnership being shaped as a counterpole to an American-Indian one. While the latter would set themselves the goal of strengthening their partnership with Japan, Pakistan, Afghanistan, and Australia, the first two - China and Russia - would extend their sights to Central Asia to safeguard the oil and gas resources there and contain Iran, with a view to gaining access to the Persian Gulf.

The two partnerships would further be enlarged by a divided Europe. Whereas some states in continental Europe view Russia as their most important, even indispensable, supplier of energy and raw material and China as their biggest market, the United Kingdom continues to be the USA's traditional ally[24] and, as such, the British government may be expected to ultimately join the American-Indian partnership. There will in all likelihood be no common policy within the European Union, leading one to assume that the EU has but little say in the process of reshaping the interplay of world powers.

In this new hegemonic situation the two blocs may be expected to establish a conflict-ridden geopolitical stability in which both sides attempt to shift the borderline between power-restricted and power-enabled freedom in their desired direction, in the process applying all the available means at their disposal. Due to the two strategic partnerships (between the USA and India and the USA and some European states on the one hand and the opposing strategic partnerships between China and Russia and some other European states on the other) requiring persistent and time-consuming techniques for balancing conflicting interests, these partnerships would necessarily have to be abandoned and replaced by a hierarchical structure on both sides of the hegemonic formation. It is most likely that the USA and China will claim leadership in this new hegemonic relation one day, and set about assuming the representation of their weaker allies.

The USA would make every effort to give the structure of the hegemonic relation a military appearance, for the simple reason that, to date, no other state has been more effective in developing and producing military technology and equipment than the USA. India would be likely to assist the USA while seeking more influence in South Asia and expecting greater defense cooperation with the American armaments industry. The Russian leaders would be keen to arm the opposite bloc, hoping that they would be able to run their armaments industry at 100 percent capacity after demonstrating their inability to convert it into a civil industry.

Just as American leaders falsely picked out Iraq as the country that would soon spearhead terrorism, China could certainly face accusations of being the most frequent violator of human rights. Quite soon, China might have to face the charge of supporting terrorism. And this despite investigations against the American Secret Service (CIA) having proved that it held some of its prisoners in secret custody and ignored international agreements against torture.

To protect the people of the world at large from these 'disgusting practices', the US government would likely claim that it is obliged to assume responsibility on behalf of the so-called 'free world,' thereby embedding the *universal term* 'freedom' in a particular American context. Many individual European governments which served the USA for more than fifty years during the former 'East-West' conflict would run the risk of being punished if they chose to revive their newly acquired awareness of independence rather than fall back on a status of being represented by "God's own country". Theories depicting the USA as the good empire (Herfried Münkler)[25] or theories on *"informal hegemony"* have already been circulating in Europe for a long time.

The leading member of the opposite bloc might easily evolve a similar strategy, thereby not only pretending that it cares for the welfare and continued existence of the entire bloc but also assigning for itself the assumed role as guarantor and overseer of the well-being of all humankind. As a result, a new 'East-West' conflict would replace the older conflict over a length of time, and in this newly formed hegemonic relation, India would stand absolutely no chance of becoming an equal partner of the USA or China.

7.2. India's triangle strategy (India, China and Russia)

7.2.1. India's interregional Asia policy
Partly overlooking the prevailing discourse of the USA being an informal hegemon, as published and backed in most Anglo-American-oriented journals of international relations, the Indian government obviously felt strong enough to pursue an interregional Asia policy. This policy intended to interlink three Asian regions - India, China, Russia - on the basis of a three-way strategic partnership between them, which extended all the way up to the Central Asian countries, the Middle East (Iran) and the European Union. The triangle strategy had the potential to change the whole interplay between the global players as one of its final consequences, and to bring about – step by step – an effective rejection of world-wide hegemony on the part of the United States.

7.2.2. Russia as a member of the Indo-Chinese strategic partnership
On the presumption that the former Soviet republics of Ukraine and White Russia would continue to be close allies of Russia, and the EU would be in a position to reject US attempts to offer Ukraine and Georgia NATO-membership, Russia's leadership had sought EU support in the past, even though it never strove for EU-membership.[26] Russia's leaders found it difficult to accept EU and NATO membership for the three Baltic states but hoped that the European Commission at least would have a moderating influence on its new members to induce them to ease their tense relations with Russia.
However, given the following worsening development, Russia changed its strategic orientation:
- The Polish und Czech governments in particular exerted an anti–Russian influence on EU foreign policy and - together with Rumania and Bulgaria - increasingly came across as vehement advocates of US interests.
- The EU put Russia down to be an unreliable supplier after the Russian company Gasprom demanded higher prices from Ukraine (which were nevertheless lower than prevailing market prices) and proceeded to interrupt its gas supply when the Ukrainian government refused to accept the company's offer.
- The EU joined the US attempt to by-pass Russia in supplying gas to Europe along the southern route, from the Central Asian states of Kazakhstan and Turkmenistan via Azerbaijan and Georgia to Turkey.
- Finland, Estonia and Sweden, all three of which border the Baltic Sea, put great obstacles to permission being granted for the Russian-German gas pipeline project to run through the Baltic Sea from Russia to Germany (Hans Gamillscheg, Ärger mit der langen Leitung, *Frankfurter Rundschau*, February 15, 2008, Schweden stoppt Pipeline, *Tagesspiegel,* February 14, 2008).
In response, Russia turned to the Chinese-Indian strategic partnership and closed the inner-regional Asian triangle by participating in it. Since then Russia and China have been keeping a watch over the gas and oil production of the Central

Asian states. Together with its ally Iran, Russia controls the Central Asian oil and gas transit routes and ensures that the only route of supply to Europe is through Russian territory. Azerbaijan has already become a party to the Russian-Iranian policy by confirming its support for the Caspian treaty.[27] The Russian-Iranian counterstrategy has succeeded in weakening American and European influence on the Central Asian states.

Apart from Europe's mistrust of Russia there was yet another reason for Russia's change of direction towards China and India. Russia had found in both countries dependable customers for its gas and oil production and has accordingly been engaged in improving its transport facilities. New pipelines have been built, railway lines upgraded, and ships for liquefied gas already pressed into service. For instance, India receives liquefied gas from Sakhalin since British Petroleum and Shell had to endure a restriction on their production rights. India and China are also very important buyers of Russian military goods. In exchange for its traditional launching base for missiles in Kazakhstan, Russia came to terms with India using an Indian base near the equator, which also served as a less expensive base for rocket launches. Both governments also agreed to build transport airplanes in a joint venture and India pledged to join the Russian navigation system, which is comparable with the American GPS.

7.3. Agreements necessary for stabilizing the strategic partnership between India, China and Russia

Firstly, none of the three partners aims at a hegemonic structure within the triangle, and differences in power are resolved through self-control and restraint on the part of the stronger partner, and self-confidence on the part of the weaker. That means the more powerful state will not anticipate service from its weaker partner. Some preliminary evidence: "India and Russia today supported their trilateral axis with China, but opposed Beijing's January 11 testing of an anti-satellite missile saying they were against militarization of space ... As Russian President Vladimir Putin held the seventh Indo-Russian summit with Prime Minister Manmohan Singh at Hyderabad House here this afternoon, it was clear that the two giant countries' decades-old-strategic ties were taken to a significantly higher level ... New Delhi and Moscow also called for expansion of cooperation within the China-Russia-India trilateral format. They noted that the first trilateral summit-level meeting, which took place in July 2006 in the outreach format of the G8 events in St. Petersburg, gave a fresh impetus to enhancing multifaceted interaction among the three states. 'The trilateral interaction promotes the development on mutually beneficial economic cooperation among India, Russia and China '...". (Rajeev Sharma, India, Russia for axis with China, *The Tribune Online Edition*, Tribune News Service. New Delhi, January 25, 2007). When India's Prime Minister received Bush at New Delhi airport in March 2007, and went on to honor Putin some months later in the same way he did Bush, he demonstrated that India does not accept any hegemonic structure, this also applying to India's relations with the US (ibid.).

Secondly, Russia provides China and India with oil and gas, and desists from preferential treatment. China's supply can be realized either by pipeline or by rail, whereas India has to be supplied oil and liquefied gas by sea from the Russian island of Sakhalin. Up to now, political hurdles have impeded the construction of pipelines from Russia and Central Asia (Kazakhstan, Uzbekistan, Turkmenistan) via Iran or Afghanistan to Pakistan and India. For instance: "The arrival of the first shipment of oil to India from Sakhalin-I in early December 2006 as well as the signing on January 25, 2007 of an MoU [Memorandum of Understanding] between ONGC [Oil and Natural Gas Corporation Ltd. India] and Rosneft [the Russian] oil company setting up two joint Working Groups -...- demonstrate the viability of future India-Russia cooperation in the entire hydrocarbon value chain" (Rajeev Sharma ibid.). China and India, to some extent, join hands in their efforts to buy oil from Sudan and other African countries.

Thirdly, Russia delivers military equipment both to China as well as India and steers clear of any preferential treatment. China understands and accepts the Indo-US civil nuclear deal, and India recognizes that China will continue to supply Pakistan with military equipment (*Hindustan Times Archives*, April 18, 2007).

Fourthly, China and India declare that there is room in Asia for the two emerging economic giants to coexist in a cooperative, rather than competitive, relationship; they are doing everything to implement this pledge in their mutual practice.

China and India have emerged as the most dynamic countries of this century. The volume of trade between India and China had touched 38.5 US dollars in 2007 and has been growing at an extremely robust rate of close to 50%. "The surge in India's imports from China is led by capital goods equipment, both mechanical and electrical. The massive infrastructure capacity built up, especially in power, is driven by Chinese imports." (Online edition of *The Economic Times*, January 15, 2008). In 2008, bilateral trade between India and China overtook that between India and its largest trading partner, the United States. The Indian Prime Minister, Manmohan Singh, recognized the market-driven agenda when he asserted that "India has no option but to engage China and give China a stake in India" (ibid.) As a consequent fallout of this assertion, the Indian government had to review its decision to bar the Hong Kong-based Hutchison Port Holdings from taking part in a project to build a container port in Mumbai due to security concerns.

India has already emerged as one of China's top ten trading partners and the rate of growth in bilateral trade has been much faster than in the case of China's other top nine partners. By 2050, China and India will be the two largest economies in the world and bilateral trade between them will become the most important economic relationship worldwide. "At the start of a symbolic visit,

President Hu Jintao of China and his Indian host, Prime Minister Manmohan Singh, unveiled a 10-point plan that aims to double bilateral trade to $40 billion by 2010. (Amelia Gentleman, China and India unveil plan for trade and cooperation, *International Herald Tribune Asia-Pacific*, November 21, 2006).
With a view to increasing their volume of trade, both countries have already opened the frontier barrier at Sikkim/Tibet. In January 2008 even the leader of the Opposition in the Lok Sabha, L.K. Advani, "advocated total normalization of relations with China, and hoped that the recent visit of Prime Minister Manmohan Singh to Beijing had brought the countries closer" (*The Hindu*, online edition, January 17, 2008).
In the above mentioned 10-point plan, India and China also "pledged cooperation in the field of civilian nuclear energy – heralding the possible end of decades of nuclear rivalry and suspicion"(ibid.) According to Ma Xiaotian, deputy chief of General Staff of the People's Liberation Army (PLA) of China, "China will continue to push forward military exchanges and cooperation with India in an effort to safeguard regional security and stability ...Military cooperation will be carried on in the spirit of mutual respect, equal consultation und mutual benefits to contribute to the building of a harmonious region with long-lasting peace and common prosperity ...Promoting military communication and cooperation will play an important role in developing [the] strategic partnership of the two neighbors, also the leading developing nations in the world." (Editor: Du Guodong, www.chinaview.cn, 2007-12-25).
Fifthly, India and China are in the process of settling their border disputes in Kashmir and Arunachal Pradesh. There have already been hidden indications of the possibility of a future agreement in which the Chinese-occupied part of Kashmir officially goes to China, and Arunachal Pradesh is acknowledged as an undisputed part of India. The leader of the Opposition in India, L.K. Advani, "appreciated the evolution of the relations in recent years and their 'constructive' approach to resolve the border question. Fully normalized relations between the two countries can become a reliable factor of peace, stability and progress both in the region and globally" (*The Hindu*, online edition, January 17, 2008).

7.4. Outlook and expansion of the India-China-Russia axis

7.4.1. Outlook

The trilateral axis brought together the two most populated countries of the world and the energy giant Russia. Even if TNCs of US-American, Japanese or European origin were to withdraw from these markets with a view to strengthening the inner-Western triangle of USA-Japan-Europe, the trade exchange between these three strategic partners would nonetheless considerably increase and give Chinese, Indian and Russian companies the chance to shore up their competitive position on the world market. Furthermore, the three partners complemented each other in a variety of products so that competition on the world market did not appear to grow into a serious problem. For instance, India complemented its intensive import of Russian energy and military goods through close cooperation in high-technology sectors (production of transport airplanes and development of a common space for travel to the moon) (Khaleej *Times online*, November 12, 2007). On the occasion of his visit to China, the new Russian President Dmitri Medvedev met the Chinese President Hu Jintao. Both presidents referred to each other as "strategic partners" and signed a treaty in which Russia pledged to deliver China a uranium enrichment factory worth over one billion US dollars (n-tv.de politik, May 23, 2008).

As additional suppliers of energy and raw material, Iran and Australia were already waiting in the doorway to conclude the membership of the inter-regional Asian market. The ASEAN states were also knocking at the door as additional trade partners (*The Economic Times*, online edition, November 18, 2007). Hundreds of billions of euros are required to improve the infrastructure in each of the three strategic-partner countries. It is therefore inconceivable for TNCs of European and Japanese origin to retreat from a market as profitable as this.

8. Iran's nuclear policy –
A political ball-game in US containment strategy?

As pointed out earlier, the Bush administration could exploit Iran's persistence on the nuclear energy front to initiate a containment policy against Russia and China. Until October 2007, many Europeans were fearful of an air-strike by Israel or the USA against Iran's nuclear installations. Israel's air force had already demonstrated its capability by destroying a Syrian military object near the border with Iraq; it had then proceeded to announce that its next attack could be aimed at a nuclear installation in Iran. The US Vice-president Dick Cheney had lent added weight to Israel's impatience with Iran's nuclear policy by holding out a similar threat, and US President George W. Bush had warned of a Third World War if Iran was not deterred from acquiring the capacity to build an atomic bomb (*Frankfurter Rundschau*, December 5, 2007, *Tagesspiegel*, October 18, 2007).

But just a month later, the U.S. National Intelligence Estimate (NIE) surprised the international community by stating that Iran had brought its atomic weapons programme to a halt way back in 2003 (Reuters-India, December 5, 2007). NIE's report hit the general public world-wide like a bomb and, consequently, Bush's warning of a direct military nuclear attack by Iran in the near future completely lost credibility. Obviously, the US secret service did not want to be the scapegoat once again.

Since then, US policy has intensified its efforts to contain Iran and, with it, all the other countries that supplied the "rogue state" with military and civil equipment besides extending it financial support.[28] In his article "More companies suspend business with Iran", published in the *International Herald Tribune* of January 17, 2008, Mark Trevelyan observes that US pressure was actually yielding results. Trevelyan mentions that recently the Ahli United Bank in Bahrain had suspended business with Iran, while the Indian oil refining company, Reliance, halted sales of gasoline and diesel to Tehran after the French banks BNP Paribas and the Calyon unit of Crédit Agricole stopped offering letters of credit, a standard payment guarantee in international trade. Trevelyan also cited a senior German banking and finance consultant as saying, "It is today impossible more or less in Europe, with a couple of exceptions, to get a letter of credit". A couple of months later, the UK-based bank Barclays also responded to US pressure and suspended all dealings with Iran's Saderat Bank and Bank Melli (*BBC News*, One-Minute World News, June 9, 2008).

At their meeting in Berlin, the six major powers (China, France, Germany, Russia, United Kingdom and USA) negotiated and adopted a draft resolution against Iran on its nuclear programme, prohibiting Iran from passing on enriched uranium to other countries (*Tagesspiegel*, January 24, 2008). The Russian minister of foreign affairs, Sergey Lavrov, was of the view that the resolution did "not have a tough sanctioning character" (*International Herald Tribune*, January 25, 2008). Indeed, the USA had not been successful in introducing hard economic sanctions. The compromise involved the voluntary surveillance of financial transactions between certain Iranian banks and the outside world and required restrictions on letters of credit, exchange of dual goods and deals with Iranian citizens closely connected with Iran's nuclear programme (*Tagesspiegel,* January 24, 2008).

As mentioned earlier, Russian and Chinese leaders shared their negotiating partner's opinion that Iran should abstain from nuclear weapons production. Therefore it did not come as a surprise when, after Iran had tested its first medium-range missile in the first week of February 2008, the Russian deputy foreign minister Alexander Losjukow "criticized the testing of a rocket and warned the country not to ignore the international community" (*Frankfurter Rundschau,* February 7, 2008, *International Herald Tribune,* February 28, 2008). At the same time, the Chairman of the International Atomic Energy Agency (IAEA) in Vienna, Mohammed El-Baradei, raised the suspicion that Iran was building a nuclear explosive device for its medium-range missiles. He demanded justification of the real purpose behind these Iranian tests with highly explosive material (*Frankfurter Rundschau,* March 5, 2008). Then in May 2008, Jossi Melman, leading contributor to the Israeli newspaper "Haaretz", warned the United States and Europe that if Iran's nuclear ambitions are not brought to an end, Israel would intervene by bombing nuclear reactors and supply-chain industries in Iran (*Tagesspiegel,* May 2, 2008). Some weeks later, the deputy chief of Israel's government, Schaul Mofas, openly threatened Iranian leaders with a military strike against Iran's nuclear equipment. He said: "If Iran continues its programme to develop nuclear bombs, we will attack" (*Tagesspiegel,* June 7, 2008).

Meanwhile, the U.N. Security Council had passed a third round of sanctions in a 14-0 vote against Iran; however, Russia and China blocked an attempt by Western nations to introduce a necessary resolution on Iran's nuclear defiance at a meeting of the U.N. nuclear watchdog agency IAEA. "Asked why Russia and China were opposed, one diplomat said Moscow decided to withdraw its support 'on principle' " (Ali Akbar Dareini, *Associated Press,* March 5, 2008). "On principle" meant that if there was no conclusive evidence of an Iranian nuclear programme to make atomic bombs, Russia and China would abstain from any vote of condemnation.

In response to Russia's and China's "on-principle" reaction, and after Iran had broken off its negotiations with the US to stabilize the internal situation in Iraq, the Bush administration switched over to a new three-pronged strategy. In a first step, Iraq's premier Nuri al-Maliki was put under pressure to attack the strongholds of the Shiite Mahdi's insurgent army at Basra and Baghdad's Shiite Sadr City. Due to large-scale support from US and British troops resulting in massive bombardments, house searches and heavy losses among the civilian population of both cities, the Mahdi army settled for a truce. After having successfully split Iraq's Shiites into opposing camps, the US army next urged the weakened Nuri al-Maliki to conclude negotiations on the "Status of Forces

Agreement" (Sofa) by July 2008. The US was of the opinion that this treaty should comprise the following demands from its side:
- Up to 50 permanent military bases without any Iraqi right to object (4 bases have already been reinforced into fortresses.);
- The right to use the armed forces against enemies without any Iraqi right to intervene;
- Complete sovereignty in Iraqi airspace up to 9200 meter above ground;
- Unlimited freedom of movement for all US troops stationed in Iraq and protection (immunity) for all soldiers and mercenaries from Iraqi justice;
- The right to arrest any Iraqi who might be considered dangerous to the US;
- Complete control of the Iraqi departments of the interior, security and defense for at least ten years and total control over Iraqi arms trade during the same period.

As per media reports, the Bush administration threatened to collect half the amount of 50 billion US dollars owed by Iraq - and blocked since Saddam Hussein became the arch-enemy of the United States - in the event of Nuri al-Maliki refusing to sign the treaty.

As a third step, the USA encouraged Iran to develop open, transparent and good-neighborly relations with Iraq, which until then had been compelled to sign the humiliating conditions of the strategic alliance with the USA. In the event of the Iranian government refusing to comply, the USA threatened to attack Iran's nuclear reactors and supply industries through US air strikes or bombardments carried out by Israel (*China View World*, June 10, 2008, Birgit Cerha, Die Angst vorm "großen Satan" and Karl Grobe, *Frankfurter Rundschau*, June 10, 2008). The as-yet-unanswered question as to whether Iran sought to construct nuclear bombs through uranium enrichment or simply intended to use nuclear power for civil purposes was regarded as being of no consequence.

Differing dramatically from US strategy, the EU and Germany in particular held on to their distinct mode of negotiation, continuing to work on Iranian leaders to convince them that cooperation was the best option (*Tagesspiegel*, June 10, 2008). In his article published in "Die Zeit" on December 6, 2007, Gero von Randow had - even at that point of time - conjectured that the Iranian leaders would demand a high price for any concession: namely, security in Iraq and in the Persian Gulf; technical know-how for the modernization of Iran's key industries and a guarantee against attempted coups. A retreat by US military ships from the Persian Gulf could be yet another move, accompanied by the abandonment of any US attempt to tap the energy resources of the Central Asian states through oil and gas pipelines laid across Iranian territory, without a peaceful settlement being reached in advance with Russia, China and all the other involved states.

9. Contradiction between India's triangle strategy and the USA's assertion of its hegemonic status

9.1. Some discord over the nuclear deal

India's strategic community had to take into consideration that American Congressmen have some problems when it comes to egalitarian thinking. For instance, some members of the American Congress, whose approval was needed for the landmark nuclear deal with India, signaled very early that agreement may be hard to obtain. US Congressman Tom Lantos, an influential Democrat in the House of Representatives International Relations Committee, announced: "New Delhi must understand how important their cooperation and support is to U.S. initiatives to counter the nuclear threat from Iran." (Patrick Goodenough, CNSNews.com International Editor, September 12, 2005: India Wants Closer Ties With US - But Also With Iran). In this context, Goodenough made a reference to the gas pipeline: "Also sensitive is the fact that the Iranian nuclear crisis is deepening at a time India and Iran have agreed to develop a pipeline to carry gas from Iran to India, via Pakistan. Washington says it opposes the pipeline project" (ibid.).

Although India's Prime Minister Manmohan Singh responded with the comment, "Individual Congressmen can say what they want - it is a free country," it remained to be seen whether, ultimately, the US would actually accept a strategic partnership between the United States and India that was on an equal footing. Only nineteen months later Siddharth Varadarajan mentioned the "Hyde Act" which "sums up obstacles in the way of implementation of nuclear agreement". Varadarajan wrote: "India feels U.S. [is] backsliding on prior commitments" (*The Hindu*, April 25, 2007). "Simply put, it does not incorporate the full set of waivers that were implicit in the July 2005 agreement when the U.S. agreed to adjust its laws" (ibid.). What really concerned the Indian government was the "right of return" (as formulated in the U.S. draft of the 123 agreement) in case the U.S.A.'s supreme national interests should be jeopardized. In accordance with the stipulated procedure, the American side "would have the right to demand the return of equipment and material supplied to India pursuant to the bilateral agreement, with compensation payable to the Indian side. This material would include any strategic fuel reserve set up with U.S. cooperation" (ibid.). On February 16th 2008, the spokesperson of the BJP (Bharatiya Janata Party), Prakash Javadekar, pointed out that contrary to the standpoint of the Indian government, the USA considered the "Hyde Act" a vital element of the Indo-US nuclear agreement. He quoted the US Secretary of State, Condoleezza Rice, who had "very clearly stated that any agreement between India and the Nuclear Suppliers Group would be acceptable to the U.S. only if it complied fully with the Hyde Act". Ms. Rice was reported to have told a panel: "It will have to be completely consistent with the obligations of the

Hyde Act" (*The Hindu*, online edition). India's concern may have been energy security but the U.S. concern was always strategic, Mr. Javadekar declared. In his opinion the primary objective of the Hyde Act was to cap India's nuclear programme (ibid.). *The Times of India* commented on the reaction of India's UPA government as follows: "The US Secretary of State's comments on the nuclear deal had 'set the cat among the pigeons in the Indian political system" (*The Times of India*, February 16, 2008). The UPA leaders had to explain to the Communist party (CPM), on whose support the UPA government depended, that in accordance with the Hyde Act, the US president retained the right to retaliate if India conducted a nuclear test. By virtue of this, the Left declared the deal already "dead" (*The Times of India*, February 21, 2008).

In a commentary on the first round of talks with the global nuclear watchdog, the International Atomic Energy Agency (IAEA), in Vienna, *The Hindu* wrote on February 24, 2008: "Pressing India to speed up implementation of the nuclear agreement, the US had recently said the negotiations with IAEA and Nuclear Suppliers Group (NSG) should be wound up by May failing which New Delhi will not get a similar deal" (*The Hindu* – News Update Service).

The Hindu mentioned that the Indian government "is working on a new template which would be more of facility-specific safeguards and take into consideration Indian interest in uninterrupted fuel supply and stockpiling of fuel as outlined in the bilateral 123 Agreement from which the deal springs" (ibid.).

In February 2008 "three influential US Senators – Joseph Biden, John Kerry and Chuck Hagel – after a meeting with Prime Minister Manmohan Singh said the negotiations with IAEA and NSG should conclude by May, failing which New Delhi will not get a 'similar' deal when the next government is formed in Washington" (*The Hindu* – News Update Service, February 24, 2008). In view of the ongoing negotiations between India and China to support India's case - before the NSG - for securing an India-specific waiver for the implementation of the Indo-U.S. civil nuclear cooperation deal, such Senatorial visits and the upcoming visit of US Defense Secretary Robert Gates are testimony to the seriousness with which US leaders assess the political situation (*The Hindu*, online edition January 17, 2008, "India seeks China's help at NSG"). Because the warning did not achieve its purpose, US Defense Secretary Robert Gates "touched down in India" and declared: "Well, I think that the civil nuclear initiative is a very good deal for both countries. We certainly are hopeful that India can get this agreement completed. But I am here independently of that, to see how we can expand the military-to-military relationship independent of the civil nuclear agreement." (*The Times of India*, February 27, 2008).

The Times of India commented on Gates' visit as follows: "It's a sign of how Washington is thinking – in terms of relations with India. While it continues to officially plug for the deal, the real shift is to see how to rescue the bilateral relationship from the debris of the nuclear deal, and somehow live for another day" (ibid.). "India says no to logistic deal with US, for now", was the title of another report in *The Times of India*. A further comment said: "Gates said his aim was to further strengthen military ties with India, which will continue to expand regardless of the fate of the civil nuclear deal, especially in the arena of arms sales and joint military exercises. The US, of course, wants to counterbalance the rapid rise of China in the region. It is also very eager to corner a major chunk of the $30 billion or so India will spend in importing weapon systems and platforms over the coming five years" (*The Times of India*, February 27, 2008).

But the Indian left-wing opposition, the Communist Party, on which India's Congress government had to rely for its majority, has so far refused to give its sanction to the nuclear deal. A day before its meeting, the Communist leader A. B. Bardhan poured cold water on any hope of a breakthrough. "As far as the Left is concerned, there is no rethink on the nuclear deal", Bardhan said (*The Economic Times*, Politics/Nation, May 5, 2008).[29] A month later the CPI(M) general secretary Prakash Karat also told the Indian foreign minister Pranab Mukherjee that "as far as getting the IAEA board of governors to approve the India-specific safeguards agreement [is concerned], the Left parties have maintained that this was not acceptable ..." (TIMES NOW, June 17, 2008). He further affirmed: "We are saying that [the] 123 Agreement should not be operationalised and our own point is that the moment IAEA safeguards are finalised after that the entire operationalisation process of the 123 gets into an auto pilot mode. India has no role to intervene because it's not a member of NSG (Nuclear Suppliers Group). It would be taken to NSG via interested parties, in this case the United States of America, and after that we do not have any check on how this process will proceed"(ibid.). After this decision it became clear that the Left parties would pull out, and in fact only the Samajwadi party voted with the government. The UPA was to be left with 284 seats, 12 more than a simple majority, enough to approve the nuclear deal and remain in power (NDTV.com – Nation, June 18, 2008). The Manmohan Singh government was now expected to notify an agreement with the IAEA in which "India undertakes that none of the items produced in the safeguard facilities shall be used for the manufacture of any nuclear weapon or to further any other military purpose" (*The Times of India* – India, July 10, 2008).

Even before the (35-nation) IAEA board of governors could wrap up the safeguards agreement and come to a decision at their 1st August meet, the members of the G8 supported the US-India nuclear deal at their meeting in Japan: "We look forward to working with India, the International Atomic Energy Agency, Nuclear Suppliers Group and other partners to advance India's non-proliferation commitments and progress so as to facilitate a more robust approach to civil nuclear cooperation with India to help it meet its growing energy needs in a manner that enhances and reinforces the global non-proliferation regime" (*The Times of India* – India, July 10, 2008). On September 11, 2008, India secured the waiver from the Nuclear Suppliers Group (NSG). The Australian Foreign Minister, Stephen Smith, attributed the granting of the waiver to three reasons: "One, even if it was a non-Nuclear Non-Proliferation

Treaty (NPT) country, it [India] was not the cause for proliferation and two was the statement of External Affairs Minister Pranab Mukherjee reaffirming India's track record on non-proliferation and commitment to disarmament" (*The Times of India,* September 11, 2008). In his opinion the third reason why the NSG changed its rule was because of "India's rise as a global power". On September 11, US-President Bush sent the text of the 123 Agreement to the US Congress for final approval and, on October 1, the Senate agreed to the Indo-US civil nuclear deal.

During her visit to India, US Secretary of State, Condoleezza Rice, sought to wrap up the 123 clause before Bush had signed the text into law. However, the Indian government insisted that all legal formalities be concluded on the U.S. side first (Siddharth Varadarajan in *The Hindu,* October 04, 2008). It clearly showed the mistrust between the two governments, while also pointing to India's policy of self-determination that resulted in special agreements being signed with Russia and France as early as in the second week of September 2008. Russia's Rosatom was to build two reactors of 1000 mw each in Tamil Nadu; France's Areva one 1600 mw reactor at Jedapur (Moneycontrol, News, Current Affairs, September 09, 2008). And in September 2008 India signaled the great importance it attached to its relationship with Russia by extending the tenure of the joint Indo-Russian panel on military and technical cooperation by another 10 years (Sandeep Dikshit in *The Hindu,* September 30, 2008).

The Indo-US nuclear deal was also of great importance to China. The Chinese government was not one of the six nations that raised objections at the NSG meeting because opposition from it could have carried the risk of pushing India closer to the USA (*Hindustan Times,* September 09, 2008). The Chinese leaders knew that although the USA steadily attempted to get India to abandon its strategic partnership with China and Russia, the Indian government continued to improve its relations with China. In May 2008, it had reversed its decision (of late 2006) not to upgrade links along the still-disputed border with China (*The Telegraph,* Calcutta, May 7, 2008) and "in Yekaterinburg, the Foreign Ministers of Russia, India and China dropped in the Harbin communiqué a dubious reference to their 'divergent interests' and 'reaffirmed the commonality in the approaches of the three countries' to global and regional problems" (Vladimir Radyuhin: The first stand-alone meeting at the Foreign Ministers level between Brazil, Russia, India and China, which was hosted by Russia, signaled a "new quality cooperation". In: *The Hindu,* May 29, 2008).

9.2. The gas pipeline project

For a long time India has been courting Iran to make progress with the gas pipeline project and had already indicated its interest in a financial stake. On 29 August 2005, representatives of both countries - the chief negotiator of the Iranian nuclear program Ali Larijani, India's Minister of External Affairs

Natwar Singh, India's Energy Secretary, and the Security Advisor M.K. Narayanan - met in New Delhi to strengthen cooperation, particularly with respect to the gas pipeline project. With respect to Iran's nuclear program, India treads extremely carefully. On December 18, 2006, Prime Minister Manmohan Singh stressed he would be the last person to plead before Parliament that India's foreign policy or its policy on Iran should be allowed to be decided in Washington or Europe. Singh pledged: "I stand by that commitment" (Seema Guha, India will not lose its nuclear swaraj: Manmohan Singh, DNA-Mumbai-Daily News&Anaysis WORLD, December 18, 2006).

During his flying visit to India in May 2008, the Iranian president Mahmoud Ahmadinejad expressed his desire to move forward in strengthening Iranian-Indian ties. Although Indian "Cassandras" like Gulshan Sachdeva, among others, warned the country that "India's image was bound to take a knock if it engaged Iran constructively in a spirit of cooperation", Ahmadinejad's visit "became a defining moment" (M.K. Bhadrakumar, Ahmadinejad's visit: a defining moment, *The Hindu*, May 10, 2008).

Bhadrakumar went on to observe: "It underscores our jettisoning of an unhappy interregnum when we adopted a neo-conservative view of Iran through the prism of our perceived 'alliance of values' with the United States" (ibid.). He also mentioned a roundtable on March 27, which brought together five former Secretaries of State: Henry Kissinger, James Baker, Warren Christopher, Madeline Albright and Colin Powell. They "reached a consensus position that the U.S. should open a Ine of dialogue with Iran" (ibid.). Consequently, Indian opinion-makers should realize that the "U.S. stratagem to isolate Iran has proved ineffectual", Bhadrakumar asserted (ibid.). Therefore, India should forge ties of friendship with Iran, a key player on the chessboard of energy security. Iran has taken the initiative for forming a cartel of gas-producing countries along the lines of the OPEC, and has already applied for membership of the Shanghai Cooperation Organization (SCO). "Also, Iran's unique location makes it a serious player in [the] surrounding regions – the Persian Gulf and West Asia, the Caucasus and the Caspian and Central and South Asia. That is why Indo-Iranian exchanges traditionally assumed a broad character" (ibid.). And India should recognize that the Iran-Pakistan-India gas pipeline project (IPI) is "doable" now. Bhadrakumar also pointed out that "India ... needs to look beyond and conceptualize how to give a multiplier effect to the impetus provided by the IPI. Beijing's offer to Tokyo of an undersea gas pipeline by way of extending its so-called 'East-West Energy Corridor' (connecting Xinjiang and Shanghai), which is under construction, leading eastward from the Caspian and Central Asia to China, is a fascinating example of how to plan ahead for the world of tomorrow" (ibid.). Bhadrakumar proposed that the IPI be extended to China (*News Post India*, April 28, 2008), and further from India to Sri Lanka, Nepal and Bhutan. India could become an energy transit country. He finally warned that India's Central Asia policy "should not remain an appendage of the U.S.' 'Great Central Asia' strategy – another neocon legacy" (ibid.). India's triangle strategy sometimes appeared to be an appendage of US strategy but that impression was wrong. Indian governments always wanted to be open towards all sides. A good example is India's intention to join the US-backed Turkmenistan-Afghanistan-Pakistan-India gas pipeline project (TAPI), declared some days before Pakistan and Iran had resolved all outstanding issues on the IPI (*Islamic Republic News Agency* (IRNA), April 28, 2008). The United States opposed the IPI and encouraged India and Pakistan to import gas from Turkmenistan. But Asian governments knew about Turkmenistan's operational treaty with Gasprom whereby its gas was to be supplied to Europe via Russian pipelines. It was also generally known that TAPI cut across the most turbulent part of Afghanistan.

The main reason for the Indian government delaying the signing of an agreement with Iran and Pakistan on the transnational pipeline project (IPI) lay in the persisting struggle over the India-US nuclear deal. On June 23, 2008, the government announced that it would sign an agreement with Iran and Pakistan "very soon" and that there were only "some minor problems" left (*The Times of India* – Gulf). Yet behind the scenes, the signing of any agreement was in reality postponed until September 2008. In the meantime, India's IPI partners exerted some pressure on the Indian government, but without any success. Washington's continuing opposition to the IPI pipeline project and the sensitive task of realizing the nuclear deal with India indicated that demands from the American leadership were incompatible with India's insistence on far-reaching autonomy.

For a long time India's strategic community simply did not appear to be used to thinking in terms of mastery and servitude. For instance India's External Affairs Minister, Pranab Mukherjee, reiterated India's commitment to global nuclear disarmament, "based on the principles of universality, non-discrimination and effective compliance", if U.S. nuclear policy avoids '"the three D's": dominance, discrimination and double standards (Inderfurth, Karl F. and Riedel, Bruce, "A U.S.-Indian partnership against nukes", *International Herald Tribune*, November 27, 2007). Another example was the Indian Defense Minister's remark on Bush's statement that the growing demand for food grains in India had led to the spiraling of global prices: A.K. Antony called it a "cruel joke" (*Hindustan Times*, May 5, 2008).

However in recent months, India's political elite appears to have changed its attitude towards the USA. Siddharth Varadarajan complained bitterly about the prevailing mindset in his article "Rising power, insecure elite" (*The Hindu*, November 10, 2008). He wrote: "This is, at one level, an extraordinary pathology. The U.S. came forward to embrace India and even offer it cooperation in the field of civil nuclear energy because it recognized New Delhi's growing capacity to affect strategic developments in Asia and the world. But far from recognizing its own strength and its ability to make a difference by being more assertive in a wide variety of arenas, Prime Minister Manmohan Singh and his Government have taken the Bush administration's embrace as an act of benevolence which needs to be repaid by active support, where politically feasible, and ambivalence or silence, when openly backing Washington might prove a hard sell domestically". Varadarajan further observed: "Maintaining the proper distance in proximity is the challenge facing Indian diplomacy in its relations with the U.S. …" In this context he pointed to the Iran-Pakistan-India pipeline to which India "could openly declare its support".

10. Europe's options - factors to be considered by the EU in evolving a suitable approach to the Asian trilateral axis

10.1. Economic interests and geo-political realities

In his article published in the weekly *Die Zeit* of October 11, 2007, Günter Hofmann pointed to the absence of a German statement on US containment policy. He confronted German leaders with the urgent question as to how the government would like to respond to US containment strategy. Actually Hofmann addressed his question to all the members of the European Union. He also proposed that the Europeans pay attention to their relationship with China and Russia in their efforts to create a balanced cooperative relationship with the USA.

Within the EU, a discussion was launched among its various members as to how to adequately respond to the new interregional Asian policy. In balancing its traditional transatlantic relations with a closer relationship towards the strengthening Asian triangle, the EU signaled that it did not intend following the US containment strategy towards China and Russia. The EU thereby challenged the hegemonic claim of the United States and consequently had to face a harsh reaction from the Bush administration. Possibly the USA retaliated by cooling off the US-EU relationship or by splitting up the various EU members into cooperative East Europeans and the United Kingdom on the one hand, and the rest of the – indignant – West European allies on the other, in the process playing one side off against the other.

Of prime importance for the EU was to clarify its position with regard to the persisting hegemonic claims of the USA. Its position had to be stated before the Bush administration attempted to initiate a US containment policy against China and Russia, exploiting Iran's persistent stand on nuclear energy and the Russian and Chinese reluctance to censure Iran's policy. A new containment policy could be implemented in a manner akin to what had been implemented in 1949, after the end of the Second World War. At that time the USA was to eventually demand Europe's involvement in the ban on exports of strategically important technology to the Soviet Union, as service in return for credit and loans extended by the Marshall Plan and goods supplied by various US companies. The USA faced the threat of exclusion from the growing inter-European barter economy primarily due to the scarcity of US dollars in Europe. Sixty years later the US administration had already lost the power to ban European exports of strategically important technology; still, it was able to threaten Europe with exclusion from the huge US market. For instance, European companies continuing to trade with the so-called rogue state of Iran were confronted with the very same US sanctions.

But German exports to China have already surpassed Germany's share of exports to the USA and, meanwhile, the EU has grown to be China's most important trading partner and Germany the center of its economic interest

(*Tagesspiegel*, April 20, 2008). For instance, the German company Siemens has already employed more than 43,000 people in China, while Volkswagen's market share in China amounts to 18.5 percent (Lague, David, in *International Herald Tribune*, November 7, 2007, *Frankfurter Rundschau*, October 27, 2007). The year 2008 has seen more than 3000 German companies engaged in China (*Tagesspiegel,* April 20, 2008). Since the year 2000, the volume of trade between China and the EU has risen by 150 percent (Eurostat, in *Tagesspiegel*, November 27, 2007). Already, the number of Chinese companies investing in Europe has been on the rise, thereby ensuring that the two trading centers are bound together by even stronger ties. Equally indispensable, as Europe's most important supplier of energy, is Russia. As already mentioned Russia, Kazakhstan and Turkmenistan agreed to construct a gas pipeline along the Caspian Sea (*Neue Züricher Zeitung Online*, May 12, 2007). The significance of this for the near future is that the two Central Asian countries will supply their gas to Europe via Russia. For the European Union there was no possibility of by-passing Russia. This was also true of the project to pump oil from Kazakhstan to Ukraine, Poland and the three Baltic states via Azerbaijan and Georgia due to the lack of a transit route across the Caspian Sea (*Frankfurter Rundschau*, October 12, 2007).

Europe's direct air traffic routes to China traditionally passed through Russia and Kazakhstan, and military transport aircraft to Afghanistan additionally had to fly over Uzbekistan. If the Russian government were to erect obstacles to the use of Russian air corridors, it would become extremely expensive for Lufthansa Cargo to take the Southern route to China via Iran, Afghanistan, Pakistan and India by way of an alternative, and if the German Army (Bundeswehr) was also debarred from taking the direct air route for its military flights to Afghanistan and had to instead choose the route via the Arab states and the Indian Ocean, each flight would become considerably more expensive. But this could occur if the German government required that Iran reconsider its nuclear policy, and the Russian government did not agree with Germany's approach towards Iran.

By way of an early warning, Russia compelled Lufthansa Cargo to move its regular stopover from Astana in Kazakhstan to Novosibirsk in Russia and forced the cancellation of a military flight to Afghanistan. After again applying for and securing permission from Russia, the military plane could then take off for Uzbekistan. Obviously there were some reasons for taking into consideration Russian interests and reactions before resorting to steps that for the most part gratified the USA.

10.2. Concrete steps in the interest of the various members of the EU

In March 2008 the German chancellor Angela Merkel traveled to Moscow to meet the outgoing Russian president Vladimir Putin and his successor Dmitri Medvedev. She expressed her hope that pending disputes between Germany and

Russia would soon be resolved. Frank-Walter Steinmeier, German foreign minister, emphasized Russia's importance for the maintenance of peace in Europe and as partner to stabilize relations among the Balkan countries; he also stressed its role in Middle East conflicts. He warned the EU against not taking Russia's concerns seriously by, for instance, thoughtlessly offering EU membership to the Ukraine. He also pronounced his reservations against Georgia being invited to become the next member of the NATO. He concluded his speech by asserting that Russia and Europe needed each other. Russia looks to Europe for its economic modernization and Europe requires Russia's cooperation for its policy of peace (*Frankfurter Rundschau*, March 6, 2008).

Germany conducted negotiations with Russia in the early months of 2008 with the aim of hammering out a transit agreement with its negotiating partner to provide the German army – which was to be stationed in Afghanistan and Uzbekistan – with non-military goods by train. As had hitherto been the case, the final treaty permitted military equipment to be transported by air using the normal transit routes via Russia. Because Russia shared with Germany a concern for the peaceful development of Afghanistan, Prime Minister Vladimir Putin even permitted military goods to be transported by rail through Russian territory in November 2008.

On the 12th of April 2008, the German foreign minister Steinmeier tried to win over his audience at Harvard University in Boston for a new alignment of the trans-Atlantic relationship. To make the world safer – Steinmeier argued – Russia should be included in efforts to enhance relations between the trans-Atlantic partners. A month later, Steinmeier set out for Moscow accompanied by several representatives of industry and the media. He met the new Russian President Dmitri Medvedev and his newly elected Prime Minister Vladimir Putin. Medvedev underlined the outstanding economic relations between Russia and Germany and called attention to the potential for further growth in bilateral relations (*Tagesspiegel*, May 17, 2008).

Just a day ahead of the RIC/BRIC (Russia, India, China/Brazil and RIC) meetings in Yekaterinburg (Russia), Steinmeier delivered a speech at Yekaterinburg's Urals University on May 13, wherein he referred to Alexander von Humboldt's visit to Yekatrinburg in 1829: Just as "Humboldt stood for the surveying of the world in the early 19th century... [a]t the beginning of the 21st century, we [also] see a new surveying of the world, albeit in a different way. With the global division of labor and the globalisation of financial markets, new horizons are opening up; and with them come enormous opportunities, but also new challenges and risks... Hundreds of millions of people, for the first time in history, have gotten the ability to generate wealth and welfare from their own strength... And what is true for the economy, is also true for politics: New power centers are emerging. In Asia, at the Arab Gulf [sic], in Latin America, even in Africa. The weights are shifting in the world. Compared to the past century, many more states and regions will influence and shape the world... The consequence is that we need more international cooperation, cross-linking and

interweavement. This necessitates a 'new thinking': Turning away [from] power politics, 'balance-of-power' politics and unilaterally pushing through national interests... For Germany and the EU, Russia is and remains the indispensable partner for building the world of tomorrow. We need Russia as the partner for security and stability in Europe and far beyond Europe." (Michael Liebig, Letter from the Rhine, Beyond the "G-8", May 22, 2008, *Solon-line* May 24, 2008). Steinmeier proposed a "partnership for modernisation" between Russia and Germany, encompassing industry, small and medium enterprises, energy, science & technology and administration (ibid.) At the joint press conference with Steinmeier on May 14, Russian Foreign Minister Lavrov said: "Russian-German relations, to which we devoted the greater part of our talks, are improving further, have – without exaggeration – a strategic character, and influence the overall situation in Europe and also in the world as [a] whole. As for Russia, with the new President and the new government, we will maintain absolute continuity in our cooperation [with Germany]" (ibid.).
With regard to the conflict between China and the exiled Tibetan political and religious leader Dalai Lama, the European Union's trade commissioner, Peter Mandelson, warned against proposals to use the Olympic Games as an instrument of protest. Boycotting the inauguration of the Olympic Games would prove ineffective and could prompt retaliation against European economic interests. "Telling the Chinese that you want to turn the Olympic Games into a fiasco and a major international embarrassment is not going to encourage the Chinese to listen", Mandelson said after a conference in London. "I don't think boycotts will get anywhere."(*International Herald Tribune*, April 16, 2008). On March 30, 2008, the EU abstained from a threat to boycott the Olympic Games (Reuters Deutschland, March 30, 2008). On the contrary, Germany in particular continued to invite Chinese journalists and train Chinese jurists.
Even the new Polish government signaled a shift in Poland's foreign policy. The new Polish foreign Minister Radek Sikorski announced that the new Warsaw government "was not prepared to accept U.S. plans to deploy part of its antiballistic missile shield in Poland until all costs and risks were considered" (*International Herald Tribune,* January 7, 2008). Three months later the Polish Defense Minister Bogdan Klich wanted the European Union "to beef up its military role by having its own independent planning headquarters and more say over military issues" (*International Herald Tribune*, April 25, 2008). However Poland permitted US-missiles to be stationed on Polish territory in October 2008.
However, the USA's most important Asian ally, Japan, improved its relations with China. China is Japan's biggest trading partner and a Japanese diplomat announced that for success in the future, Japan and China needed good relations with each other (*Tagesspiegel*, December 29, 2007). The outcome of these developments was that the European governments responded positively to the extended Asian triangle of Russia-China-India and reviewed their traditional transatlantic relations.

The Bush administration recommended that the Europeans join hands with the US in implementing its containment strategy, but until now this has had little effect. For instance an article written by David Shambaugh and published in the *International Herald Tribune* carried the title "A love affair gone sour" – "Positive European perceptions of China have dropped dramatically over the past year" (*International Herald Tribune*, November 27, 2007). On the other hand, as has already been revealed, most of the EU members tried to handle the Tibet question very carefully and were even eager to redress economic imbalances through new trade agreements.

In April 2008, the US President George W. Bush tried to prod the NATO summit meeting in Bucharest (Rumania) into welcoming Georgia and Ukraine into the Membership Action Plan which prepares nations for NATO membership. Referring to the democratic revolutions in both Ukraine and Georgia, he said: "Welcoming them into [the] Membership Action Plan would send a signal to their citizens that if they continue on the path to democracy and reform they will be welcomed into the institutions of Europe" (*International Herald Tribune* Europe; April 2, 2008). By his surprise move he upset some of his NATO allies. For instance, the German ambassador to London, Wolfgang Ischinger, while commenting on Bush's initiative said that "not enough diplomacy had taken place beforehand with Russia" (ibid.) Ronald Asmus, a key figure in the Clinton administration said that "Bush's speech set up a dramatic battle that will be fought out over the next two days and whose outcome will be important in shaping his legacy, and America's diplomatic standing in the alliance" (ibid.). This resulted in a tense atmosphere, and finally Germany and France stalled Bush's project and even Bush's closest ally, the British Prime Minister Gordon Brown, did not fully back the American plan. The rejection was a considerable blow to Bush, and the Russian President Putin, who attended the meeting as a guest, was declared winner of the stand-off by the NATO members. This defeat demonstrated the USA's downslide from an undisputed leader to just an ordinary NATO member; besides it indicated that the USA faced the risk of becoming isolated.

11. The Isolation of the USA

11.1. A flawed perception

What were the consequences for the structure of international relations that resulted from a weaker USA? Were the members of the US political and economic establishment capable of dealing with the rapidly deteriorating conditions? Who could help US strategists adjust to a realignment in power relations? Only the United Kingdom appeared to be still allied with the USA. Virtually all the other former friends of the USA looked to pursue, or already pursued, their own policies and merely paid lip service to the US. Asked whether at present the USA or Russia is the more dangerous of the two for international relations, Germany's former chancellor Helmut Schmidt surprisingly pointed to the US (*Zeit-Magazin Leben* 47/2007, p. 62). Russia's former President Vladimir Putin surmised that the USA only needs vassals it can boss around (*Frankfurter Rundschau*, December 21, 2007).

Despite such conspicuously negative perceptions, the Carnegie Endowment's neo-conservative expert, Robert Kagan, defended Bush's unilateral course and asserted that the American President's policies were in tune with the US' general perception of its role in the world. In his opinion, US foreign policy was guided by two basic motives. The first was to establish the USA as a power that works for the good of the world. The second was the desire to remain the most powerful nation of the world, forever willing to bring into play its military might, even when the rest of the world is opposed to it (*Die Zeit*, January 10, 2008). Kagan therefore argues that a war between the USA and China is possible if a double strategy of co-operation and containment does not yield adequate results, and the threat of regime change remains the last means of exerting pressure on China (*Die Zeit*, January 17, 2008).

Instead of focusing on the imminent isolation of the USA, Kagan has thus turned his gaze more intensely on a great anti-China coalition, assuming that Japan, Europe and India would support the USA in a war against China.[29]

11.2. Financial crisis and massive indebtedness

11.2.1. A blow to the self-image of US-Americans

Over and above any realignment in the global interaction of powers, the USA faces the threat of becoming isolated. Holding out the threat of isolation is the financial crisis in the US and its massive indebtedness. The country is encumbered by rising household debt and a trade deficit; in future, it would be even less capable of absorbing the export goods produced by the rest of the world.

In the opinion of Joseph Stiglitz, the economic downturn was the immediate consequence of the Iraq war (*Welt-Online/Politik*, Stiglitz. Wir werden teuer für den Irak-Krieg bezahlen, May 3, 2008). Before the USA went to war in Iraq, the oil price had hovered around $ 25 per barrel. In the meantime the price per barrel has shot up to more than $ 150 and, in Stiglitz' reckoning, the war had been the main contributory factor for this rise. But Stiglitz is wrong in his pronouncement that the Iraq war has been the first to be financed by foreign countries since US independence. He has overlooked the Gulf War ten years ago, which both Germany and Japan had co-financed. In the case of the present Iraq war, the liberating and occupying powers, USA and the UK, had wanted to be paid through oil deliveries from a liberated Iraq. However, due to the pipelines having been reduced to a state of destruction and disrepair, only a tiny fraction has been paid so far, so that in reality, it is China that has been faced with the threat of having to pay, mainly as a result of the depreciating value of its US treasury bonds.

The devaluation of the US currency meant more than a blow to the self-image of the Americans: it undermined the US dollar's position as the premier reserve currency, while a switchover to the euro as a second world reserve currency competing with the US dollar was foreseeable. Burgeoning household debts and an only marginally falling trade deficit were indicative of the growing weakness of the US economy. "The jobs destroyed by international trade are far more salient than those it creates" observed Alan S. Binder in the *International Herald Tribune* of January 7, 2008 – a dilemma that also resulted in Americans losing faith in globalization, once regarded as an indispensable source of US strength.

11.2.2. Some indicators for identifying a crisis
Looming ahead is a general economic crisis, when real production and financial economy drift in different directions and the circulation of financial capital is no longer even backed by the production of goods. The following sections contain some indicators for identifying a crisis:

11.2.2.1. More profit from financial investment than from the production
of goods

If in an economy capital yields more profit through financial investment than through the production of goods, the modernization of factories initially slows down, to then take a complete downturn. There is a threat of unemployment accompanied by dwindling private consumption, which tends to increase if companies are not able to compete with the more advanced production of goods in other economies.

But against the backdrop of globalization, capital invested in the production of goods can yield more profit in some economies while financial investment may be more profitable in others. For instance, capital invested in new Chinese, Indian, Brazilian, Mexican or Vietnamese industries may be extremely lucrative while at the same time, capital investment in established industrial countries or regions like USA, Europe or Japan is also profitable. The sum total of profits and dividends increases capital flows already circulating around the world, and tends to widen the existing gap between the volume of goods produced across the world and the size of financial investment worldwide.

In aspiring to satisfy their clients' pursuit of profit, investment bankers are inclined to widen the range of opportunities in stock broking and create completely new, complex derivative instruments.

As a result, stockbrokers treat the new derivatives as a normal component of their day-to-day business, similar to normal credit swaps, with a view to inventing new credit-based money. Finally, a sum of money, multiplied several times over, circulates between the various stock exchanges and, due to an unknown volume of subprime credit added, no one is able to assess the real value of the massive amount of credit-based money. The increased gap between the volume of goods produced and the enormous amount of financial investment puts the credibility of financial businesses at risk and has an undermining impact on mutual trust. Eventually, the devastating nature of the consequences will culminate in an economic crisis.

11.2.2.2. Speculation in falling or rising exchange rates of currencies

National and transnational companies operating in diverse markets, thereby often obliged to rely on future transactions, have to deal with various currencies and their permanently shifting exchange rates. In their effort to immunize themselves against fluctuations in exchange rates, they are compelled to purchase the requisite currencies in advance and also sell an equal amount at a future date. This business further encourages stockbrokers to speculate on falling or rising exchange rates, as a result of which, for instance, over three billion US dollars are presently being shifted between the various foreign exchange markets. Add to this the billions of euros, sterling, Swiss francs and other more or less freely convertible currencies that have been transferred. Since money circulation always tends to get divorced from the underlying production of goods, this sort of currency speculation can also create a pernicious gap between both the spheres which invariably gives rise to inflation.

11.2.2.3. Shareholder attitude and investment in land, houses, commodities and the financial market

Demands for huge profits as a result of shareholder attitude – profits appropriated at the expense of wage-earners – give rise to a widening gap in income between holders of assets and recipients of wage income. If, additionally, the spending power of the gainfully employed drops, stockholders refrain from investing their money in the production of goods and increasingly switch over to other sources of income by, for instance, acquiring land and houses, speculating in commodities such as gold, oil and agricultural products, and investing in the financial market, all of which hold out the promise of higher profits. Such speculation is often likely to create bubbles, as for instance in the first months of 2008 when the price of oil soared sharply at a time when the major economies were already entering into a recession. The longer the speculation, the bigger the bubbles and the sharper the fall after the first signs of a drop in prices induce speculators to withdraw their money in panic-driven haste.

11.3. Some reasons for the US financial crisis

11.3.1. 'Failure at a lot of levels'

Home loans to risky borrowers were the first to go bad in the US economy, but the crisis also had several other reasons. A Goldman spokesman said: "At the center of the boom in mortgages for borrowers with weak credit was Wall Street's once-lucrative partnership with subprime lenders. This relationship was a driving force behind the soaring home prices and the spread of exotic loans that are now defaulting in growing number" (Jeny Anderson/Vikas Bajaj, Subprime scrutiny focuses on Wall Street, in: *International Herald Tribune*, December 7, 2007). As for instance in the case of Mrs Lakeisha Williams, whom a First Metro mortgage agent persuaded to buy eight houses on credit. Although he knew she only had a low income as assistant helper in an old people's welfare home, he convinced her to raise mortgages and let her unscrupulously run up a debt of nearly one million US dollars. Her creditors were three of the nine most important commercial banks which specialized in subprime credits (Kohlenberg, Kerstin, Acht Häuser für Lakeisha, *Die Zeit*, February 14, 2008).

Thus, once house buyers found the progressive increase in their home-loan interest rates no longer written off by the rising value of their properties, they were unable to collect the remaining loans whereupon the non-performing loans had to be combined with other credit instruments so that they could be traded on the global financial market despite their reduced value. Together with the unbridled increase in derivative products (Collateralized Debt Obligations [CDOs], Asset backed Securities [ABS], Credit Default Swaps [CDS]) [30] in all the remaining areas of business of investment banks, this not only set the stage for unlimited capital investment opportunities but also enhanced the risk of both institutional and private capital investors being infected with dubious instruments worldwide. For, in the last decade, the overriding aim of US governments and the Federal Reserve had been to maintain creditworthiness while at the same time retaining a firm hold over global finance policy, even though the country lived well beyond its financial means, leaving its creditors with little hope of loans being repaid. There emerged a linkage that was even paradoxical: the greater the proportions its debt assumed, the more unassailable the US government grew in the eyes of its numerous creditors. For, if the creditors were to redeem their low interest-bearing US treasury bonds in US dollars on a larger scale, they would risk a sharp fall in the dollar, thereby triggering off a global recession.

To retain the creditors' confidence in the US dollar despite the continued state of indebtedness, it was absolutely necessary to continuously boost the American economy, particularly the – for the most part – credit-financed consumption in the USA as well as the growing state demand for military arms, likewise financed through credit. The creditors would then – so the speculation goes – finally even be ready to include in their portfolios loan receivables whose origins were dubious and whose real value was extremely suspect.

Alan Binder, former vice-chairman of the Federal Reserve and currently professor for economics at Princeton, said: "It's a failure at a lot of levels. It's hard to find a piece of the system that actually worked well in the lead-up to the bust." (Nelson D. Schwartz/Julie Creswell, Desperate for solution, but who understands the problem?, *International Herald Tribune*, March 25, 2008). This fundamental failure could be attributed to the deregulation policy of the US Congress and the Republican and Democratic administrations over the past decade – a policy known by the term "neo-liberalism" and regarded as one of the important instruments for building US global hegemony.

11.3.2. The overriding aim to globalize US hegemony

On March 17, 2008, James Dimon, CEO of JP Morgan Chase admitted: "We have a terribly global world and, over all, financial regulation has not kept up with that" (ibid.). But the words "kept up" still constitute an understatement. Financial regulation did not include Wall Street at all. Barney Frank, chairman of the Financial Services Committee of the House of Representatives, complained that "not only did Wall Street have so much freedom, but it gave commercial banks an incentive to try and evade their regulations" (ibid.). With reference to Wall Street he admitted that the House of Representatives "thought we didn't need regulation" (ibid.). Wall Street bitterly opposed any attempt to regulate the emerging derivates market, as Michael Greenberger, a former senior regulator at the Commodity Futures Trading Commission, recalled (ibid.). He also mentioned Allan Greenspan, former chairman of the Federal Reserve, who "felt derivatives would spread the risk in the economy" (ibid.). "In reality", Greenberger added, "it spread a virus through the economy because the products are so opaque and hard to value" (ibid.).

Those are the reasons why a "stealth market" emerged based on "trades conducted by phone between Wall Street dealer desks, away from open securities exchanges" (ibid.). Any attempt to regulate this market was fought by politicians, "arguing that it would force the lucrative business overseas" (ibid.). In other words, the unregulated American market was obviously considered essential for promoting the overriding objective of globalizing US hegemony.

11.3.3. The fragile structure of the "global financial architecture"
(Geoffrey Underhill)

Several months prior to these first signs of a financial crunch, Geoffrey Underhill and other experts were already concerned about the fragile structure of the "global financial architecture" (GFA), its "lack of effectiveness and political legitimacy in a wide range of countries" (Underhill, Geoffrey R.D., "Policy Recommendations", Section 1: "Concerning the shareholder principle specifically", in: *Global Financial Architecture, Legitimacy, and Representation: Voice for Emerging Markets*, Garnet Policy Brief, No. 3, January 2007). Underhill defined "financial architecture" as "the sum of international institutions and co-operative processes aimed at managing global imbalances, exchange rates, transnational capital flows, and financial market stability, from crisis prevention to management to debt workout".

According to Underhill, traditionally, financial policy-making took place in relatively closed communities in which central banks, finance ministries, regulatory agencies and their private sector interlocutors interacted. In his opinion, cross-border market integration had additionally brought in powerful private actors, "in particular large internationally-active financial institutions" which tend to undercut the democratic-based decisions of state institutions (ibid.). As a result, nowadays, policy would be "based more on economic theory than on the facts of the matter, and policy therefore needs to be better grounded in the real word" (ibid.). Politicians should concentrate on reforms "directly confronting the political underpinnings and distributional impact of the financial architecture, especially with respect to a) who decides, in whose interest? b) the legitimacy of both decision-making processes and the policies that result and c) the links between the decision-making process and the outcome." (ibid.).

Underhill's criticism was vehement: "Cross-border financial integration results in a considerable tension between what national policy makers are required to do in a democratic context and what they actually can do in the face of global financial constraints" (ibid.). He recommended: "We ... need to think about **who** is included in the process, how a broad underlying consensus might be built, and thereby how to enhance the legitimacy of the outcome through sound policies appropriate to a wider range of interests, eventually building longer-term diffuse support for global financial governance" (ibid.). After the financial crunch grew apparent, the room for trustworthiness shrank drastically and was taken over by wide-spread resentment, mainly because predominantly illegitimate and undemocratic methods were opted for on both sides in the equation between the input of the policy process and its output.

For a long time, US administrations did not accept any rationale that urged them to follow Underhill's proposals. For instance, the USA reacted with a lack of understanding when Europeans proposed a reform of the International Monetary Fund (IMF). In this case Geoffrey R.D. Underhill had recommended that "the US must think seriously about an eventual end to its effective veto over amendments to the Articles; this should be traded off against a combined if sufficiently reduced EU vote where neither would claim a veto."[31] Even after the crunch had taken a serious turn and countries were "effectively 'checking out' of the Hotel Capital Mobility", the USA clung to its veto right. US voting power still accounts for 16.77 % of the total. Obviously only an alliance between the

Asian triangle, the European Union, the Arab Emirates, Japan and Brazil could force the US administration to change its unacceptable position. Until now the US' privileged status, which permits it to get into unlimited debt in its own currency, has remained inviolate. To date, no other member state of the Bretton Woods' institutions enjoys the same advantage. So far there has been a great deal of criticism but no fundamental questioning.

Even China as the largest creditor and the European Union as the most important competitor to the US on the world market are yet to take any decisive steps. On the contrary, China tried to circumvent the negative effects of a depreciating US dollar by switching over from the US dollar to the euro and improving its interest account, for instance by getting a foothold in US banks and investment companies like Blackstone, one of the leading US American investors which calls itself "the leading global alternative asset manager and provider of financial advisory services" (Blackstone Group website). The European Union created the euro as a serious challenger to the U.S. dollar, but for a long time has had no sustained success in replacing the U.S. dollar as an accounting currency for raw material (oil, gas etc.) and high-value goods (such as airplanes).

Not until US investment and commercial banks were forced to announce huge losses, and not until the mayors of several US cities were faced with a drastic fall in property taxes, forcing them to reduce their spending, did the US government feel in any way obliged to deal with the mounting financial crisis. After one of the leading investment banks, "Bear Stearns", which was insolvent and close to bankruptcy, had to be rescued by a government-brokered deal with JP Morgan, the US Treasury pushed through a plan to subordinate Wall Street to a new regulatory apparatus of the nation's financial system. The bailout of Bear Stearns indicated that there was no time left for the US government and the Federal Reserve System to create a regulatory umbrella exclusively for the US financial market. The Swiss banker, Oswald Grüber, described the intervention as a measure that prevented the international financial system from going bankrupt (*Frankfurter Rundschau*, April 21, 2008).

Meanwhile, Wall Street executives in particular had come under pressure from shareholders for their mounting subprime-related losses. Robert Steel, Under Secretary of the US Treasury and former Goldman Sachs executive, promoted a new Treasury plan to regulate Wall Street business in April 2008 (Landon Thomas Jr., Learning to embrace regulation, *International Herald Tribune*, April 16, 2008). Steel made it known that as per the plan, the Treasury "will have the licence to go everywhere: private equity funds, investment banks, hedge funds" (ibid.). A month earlier, the Federal Reserve System had already accepted mortgage certificates with top-rating in exchange for credits, mainly in order to rescue Fannie Mae and Freddie Mac, the two most important banks that specialized in buying mortgage loans issued by smaller banks and selling them on the financial market.

Although various state-owned funds from China, the Arab Emirates and Singapore had already engaged in the US financial market and invested in some US banks (Citigroup, Merrill Lynch, Morgan Stanley) which had run into difficulties[32] (*Frankfurter Rundschau*, January 15, 2008), the following US banks accumulated huge write-downs and credit-related costs running into several billion US dollars till April 2008 because of the unknown value of the structured products in their portfolio which were difficult to sell or could not be sold at all: Citigroup, the largest commercial US bank; Bank of America Corp., the second-largest US commercial bank; JP Morgan Chase, the third-largest commercial bank; Morgan Stanley, the second-largest US investment bank; Wells Fargo, the second-largest mortgagee and Lehmann Brothers, a smaller investment bank.

Undoubtedly, leading European banks, foremost among them the two Swiss banks USB and Credit Swiss, but also Deutsche Bank and some state-owned German banks were severely affected by the credit crunch but most of them were far from losing their license. This was however to be the fate of a British bank. At first the UK government bailed out *Northern Rock* and subsequently the bank had to be nationalized. The City of London suffered greatly from the credit crunch and many employees even lost their jobs. "An unprecedented 50 billion pound injection to bail out Britain's ailing banking system could even be doubled if it fails to stave off a collapse in the housing market", the *Times* reported (*Thomson Financial News*, Forbes, April 21, 2008).

The effect of the US financial crisis on Wall Street as the – hitherto – most important center of financial transactions has been extremely severe. The total amount of write-downs caused by the US financial crisis until April 2008 was reckoned to be as much as 945 billion US dollars (*Frankfurter Rundschau*, April 9, 2008), which raised the question as to whether the USA had lost all credibility and already gambled away the last pillar that supported its status as a hegemonic power.

11.3.4. Simply "New Modes of Behavior" or a veritable "New Deal" ?

To protect the USA from a precipitous fall, leading US economic experts and the architects of Bush's deregulating economic policy, such as Matthew Slaughter, have for years even talked about a "New Deal" aiming at "an aggressive redistribution of income" (Harald Schumann, Wer rettet die Globalisierung? *Tagesspiegel*, April 20, 2008). Once again the state was called upon to rescue the market economy. At the expense of the tax payer, the Federal Reserve System was expected to accept unsaleable structured products and, at a later point, the state was to initiate a Keynesian economic policy (Mark Schieritz, Genug diskutiert! *Die Zeit*, March 13, 2008). In the meantime, the European currency further improved its value against the US dollar and touched 1.6 US dollars to the euro. The euro may be expected to develop into the second most important reserve currency after the US dollar. Showing a surprising

readiness to talk about tax havens, the United Kingdom took a first cautious step towards de-linking the former Anglo-American alliance.
Martin Wolf realized that "the public, (as) governments feel, must be protected from banks, and banks must be protected from themselves. Finance is deemed far too important to be left to the market". He concludes that "regulation will always be highly imperfect. But an effort must still be made to improve it" (Wolf, Martin, Seven habits that finance regulators must acquire, *Financial Times*, May 7, 2008).
Drawing on Nouriel Roubini of New York University's Stern Business School, Martin Wolf proposed seven principles of regulation and called them the seven "Cs":
1. *coverage*: "Regulatory coverage must be complete. All leveraged institutions above a certain size must be inside the net." (ibid.)
2. *cushions*: Availability of sufficient "equity capital" and "liquidity"
3. *commitment*: "Originators" should "care sufficiently about the quality of loans they plan to offload on to others" (ibid.)
4. *cyclicality*: Rules should be contra-cyclically designed
5. *clarity*: To avoid, for instance, a "conflict of interests" in the functioning of rating agencies
6. *complexity*: Since excessive complexity is a "significant source of lack of clarity", the need for "all derivates (to) be traded on exchange".
7. *compensation*: To avoid "symmetrical losses".

"The mantra of aligning incentives seems to be lost in the failure to impose symmetrical losses – or frequently any loss at all – when failures ensue" (Paul Volcker). Finally, Wolf cited John Maynard Keynes: "When the capital development of a country becomes a by-product of the activities of a casino, the job is likely to be ill done". Beyond these principles, fiscal policy should be mindful of yet other proposals put forth by Keynes, if the credit crunch is not to end in a veritable economic crisis. Cushy, self-indulgent proposals that one just need hang around and do nothing as long as the loss of 1000 billion US dollars is written off (International Monetary Fund) pass the burden on to the tax payers and the unemployed who have lost their jobs during an economic crisis. What is risky but more humane is the redistribution of income and wealth within the framework of a re-enacted "New Deal". In the face of disturbances and even revolutionary developments it could be a much-needed measure to maintain social peace (Blomert, Reinhard, Keynes' Idee vom Glück, *Tagesspiegel,* Mai 25, 2008).

11.4. Plan B for maintaining US hegemony

In his article „U.S. follows lead of Europeans in supporting banks" published in the International Herald Tribune on 15th October 2008, Floyd Norris revealed how, despite the financial market being infested with bad loans and dubious derivatives and the global crisis this has engendered, American financial capital would like to retain the pre-eminent position it has held since decades. Competing with the USA were the 15 European euro states as well as the USA's biggest creditors today – China, Japan, the oil-producing Arab states, Russia and Brazil. The main allies of the United States on the other hand were globally operating transnational companies and financial organizations, whose day-to-day business in no inconsiderable measure involved their efforts to secure returns on their capital investment. Given the above scenario, the United Kingdom with its financial center in London, whose position in the past decades rested on Wall Street's well-being, found itself caught in between, as were the state investment funds which had stakes on both sides. The approach outlined by Norris could be called „Plan B"; it followed in the wake of the failed „Plan A".

11.4.1. „Plan A" – the historical run-up to the present financial crisis
„Plan A" operated on the following basis: the world's biggest debtor determines developments on the financial markets and dictates the run of things to anti-American central banks and governments. With the Bretton Woods Agreement of 1944 presenting the USA with the option of borrowing, the country, over the decades, ran up a colossal mountain of debt. In doing so, the USA always gave priority to adequate liquidity being infused into the global financial system, whilst all the other countries regarded the USA's leadership role with increasingly mixed feelings.
- Thus, after the end of the Vietnam War (1973), once gold backing for the US dollar was removed, the exchange rate freed and the euro dollar – traded on the London stock exchange – came into being, the USA created a „sister currency" under its overall control through which the global financial system was to be infused with additional liquidity.
- In the 1980s, when the stock market plunged by 20% during the savings and loan crisis, and the call for greater liquidity was sounded before the re-regulation of the savings and credit market, Alan Greenspan, the new chairman of the Federal Reserve appointed by President Reagan, ensured a further spurt in liquidity through his *cheap money policy*.
- With the end of dual hegemony between the USA and the Soviet Union in the beginning of the 90s and the rise of the US as the sole global hegemonial power in the age of the new information technology and the US-promoted globalization of the markets, Greenspan[33] strove to meet the requirements of the growing flood of investment-seeking capital and the massive rush for dividends closely linked thereto through newly created derivatives. On his recommendation, President Clinton signed a law that exempted US-American investment banks from any kind of regulation, while the introduction of ever-new derivatives gave the banks the opportunity to create an unlimited amount of liquidity. It was this law that set the stage for the commencement of an unrestricted debt policy on the part of the USA.

- In order to retain the creditors' confidence in the US dollar despite continued indebtedness, it was absolutely necessary to keep the US economy continuously boosted, particularly the predominantly credit-funded consumption of American consumers and the likewise credit-financed increase in state demand for military arms. It was speculated that creditors dependent on the USA would finally be ready to even include in their portfolio demands for loans whose origins were dubious and whose real value extremely questionable.

In view of the dramatic situation that is taking shape, the following questions may be posed: Did one perhaps hope that non-American banks would be the first to be affected if the infectious bubble were to finally burst?

- Commercial banks located in economies of low financial strength, at first nourished and later encumbered and tainted by collateralized debt obligations and credit default swaps, would face insolvency sooner or later.
- Financially well-backed US banks would kindly proffer their methods of crisis management to the collapsing banks.
- In return, the bailed out banks would be called upon to adopt US banking rules and accept their partner's dominance and, gradually, Wall Street would gain greater control over the global financial market.

There have been some indications that US strategy pointed in that direction. For instance, as in the early stages of the financial crisis, the German bank IKB (Deutsche Industriekreditbank) asked for financial support due to its staggering burden of accumulated US junk credits. US banks shrugged off the bank's dangerous predicament as an exclusively German problem, refusing to admit that its origins lay in the deregulated US financial market.

Had financially sound US investment and commercial banks therefore speculated that they would patronizingly offer collaborating banks their help in overcoming liquidity problems? Objections from the European governments who struck a note of caution at the G-7/8 Summit were at any rate dismissed by the Bush administration in consensus with the Bush government as long as there was obvious hope that the bulk of the bad loans would actually accumulate with banks outside the financial centers of Wall Street and London City. It was only when there was growing realization that the bulk of the infected loans would flow back to the USA and would predominantly circulate between the 10 largest American banks that it became clear to those responsible for this crisis that they would ultimately be the ones left to bear the brunt of the consequences arising from these bad loans and dubious derivatives.

In this context, certain political events could also be regarded as foreign policy and military tactics employed to divert attention:

- The attempt to isolate China by challenging Chinese rule over Tibet (in the context of the Olympic Games in Beijing)
- The instrumentalization of the Iranian and Georgian conflicts with the aim of isolating both Iran and Russia and
- The stationing of missiles in Poland with the aim of vitiating Poland's relations with the EU and Russia.

However, when these areas of conflict obviously failed to divert attention in the long term, "Plan A" was doomed to fail. "Plan B" had to follow "Plan A" if Wall Street and London City were to retain their dominance over their competitors in the realm of global finance.

11.5. "Plan B" – Useful results of a controlled breakdown

11.5.1. Crisis management measures for preventing the financial crisis from spinning out of control

An uncontrolled global financial crash would not only bring lasting disrepute to the two most important financial centers, Wall Street and London, but also have a ruinous impact on the real economy. The warning sent out by the Great Depression of 1929 and the counterproductive monetary policy of the central banks at the same time drove the US and British governments to act speedily to overcome the crisis. For, ultimately it was Anglo-American dominance in global financial business, transacted until then through the two financial centers of New York and London, and the predominantly British-controlled tax havens which were at stake.

The question that was cause for anxiety for all the banks, namely whether the traditional trading partners in their necessary day-to-day inter-bank business were still solvent or perhaps close to insolvency, only increased suspicion among the banks. Within a short while, inter-bank trading as a whole came to a halt; in "normal times" it served, in the short term, to re-finance commitments made for the longer term. Central banks jumped into the fray and supplied the money market with "fresh money" by offering the sick banks the unsaleable bad loans for purchase and packaging their traditional money market instruments attractively to woo potential borrowers. In cases where all other bailout packages threatened to fail, the state itself entered the scene with offers of nationalization so as to either pass on the entire accumulated tax burden to the taxpayer with immediate effect (as opposed to the hitherto prevalent neo-liberal-oriented refusal on the part of the state) or to merely help out with indemnity bonds in serious cases.

11.5.2. The demand for the regulation of the financial markets

The rising discussion on regulation proposals saw the requirement for the mandatory disclosure of information by the creditors being supplemented by the order that the creditors remain responsible for a certain percentage of the loans sanctioned. Some states had already banned so-called short sales in derivatives trading in which the insolvency of the original borrowers was speculated. There were also heated discussions on the drastic cuts in manager salaries and the scrapping of the bonus system.

With regard to the demand both for suitable institutions for regulating the financial markets and expedient regulatory measures, there were some who complained about the proven inadequacy of intra-market control mechanisms and campaigned for the intervention of the regulating state, while others in turn sought to divest the state of its power to control the market, instead reposing their confidence in the – merely state-backed – self-regulating measures of financial players. These conflicts were fought against the background of varying perceptions of the state. It is well-known that in its perception of the state, the USA differed radically from continental Europe [34].

11.6. Regulation against the background of varying perceptions of the state

The state had been existing in various forms long before the emergence of civil society; thereafter it continued to exist alongside civil society as an independent pole in its own right, with its own weight and standing, at no point perceiving itself as a mere derivative of civil society. Particularly in the national societies of continental Europe that emerged after the fall of absolutism, the state never lost its exclusivity. The basis of the authority of the state in the constitution (Basic Law) of the Federal Republic of Germany and the interpretation of this article in the Bonn Commentary of the Basic Law clearly prove that very little importance was given to the sovereignty of the people and to society while tracing the source from which the state derived its authority.

Although the state in the Basic Law no longer derives its authority from God but from the people (Article 20, Para II, Sentence I of the Basic Law of the Federal Republic of Germany ["All state authority emanates from the people"]), there is "no legal relationship between the people and parliament, because the people constitute a legal entity to which rights and duties may be assigned only within the state and not on their own..." (The Bonn Commentary of the Basic Law, vol. 6, p.26). "This view", as postulated by the commentators of the Basic Law "...does not amount to disregard for political facts (...) but is the result of the distinction between a political idea and its realization in positive law" (ibid. p.26). Constructing a legal relationship between the people and parliament on the basis of the ideological conceptions of the real 'wielder' of state power is, in the opinion of these commentators, to be "rejected". In other words: the people were at no time considered the actual "wielders" of state authority. The sentence that all state authority emanates from the people is virtually turned on its head when state authority as the highest authority "emanates" not from the people themselves but from an "unorganised", "unformed" "politically ideational unit" which is "constantly in a state of flux, from the point of view of both "material and personnel resources", but which nevertheless is expected to be present as a "tangible intellectual whole" ("konkret geistige Ganzheit"). Embedded in a history of ideas and divorced from the relevant social background of the evolution of such ideas, underlying assumptions such as that of Rousseau's general assembly of people turn into axioms that are no longer challenged, serving only to legitimize the established distribution of power.

All the same – despite the sovereignty of the people being relegated to the background, the ideologically conditioned re-linking of state authority to a general assembly of people does – in a certain respect – have a substantial impact. The state authority would do well to always respect the assumed initial equality of all participants of the general assembly and to give adequate expression to this in its decisions. This has particular relevance during times of crisis when social peace stands jeopardized, and the choice of measures for its restoration is fought over in the course of the struggle between different social groups. Thus, there is for instance an absolute lack of understanding among low-wage earners and the long-term unemployed for the generous support extended by the state to banks threatened by lack of liquidity, without these banks expected to reciprocate by way of adequate performance, whereas on the other hand there is generally no bottomline fixed for low wages through the fixing of a minimum wage, and Hartz IV recipients are subjected to strict, humiliating controls. Such glaring disparities in treatment only provoke angry reactions, violate the imperative of equality and threaten social cohesion and harmony.

On the other hand, in a society that has evolved from settler communities as in the USA, the "people as a whole" are *not* looked upon as the source of state power. The axiom of people's sovereignty has no significance. The individual who acts on his own free will does not cede his primordial freedom to the state, for settler communities insist that each and every member retain the ability to fully tap the latent talents within and is subjected to minimum control. Settler communities protect themselves and their property by developing and defending common values in both unwritten and written agreements. It is only when it comes to issues extending beyond the scope of individual settler communities or involving protection from external enemies that these communities feel obliged to establish the supra-community institution that is the state and equip it with sufficient funds. In order to preserve the freedom originally bestowed upon the individual, the settler communities permit the state administration to only operate within narrow limits.

However, the older settler communities get, the greater the possibility that disparities in income and assets emerging over time as a result of differences in living conditions will give rise to situations where representative bodies and state administrations are not only confronted with widely diverging interests but also put to use by the privileged sections of the population in pursuit of their own interests. The privileges secured are however basically accepted by all individuals as a result of their primordial freedom being restored. They do not violate any precept of equality but are regarded as the consequence of the primordial freedom practiced by every individual with varying degrees of success. Even where such a privilege-promoting state acts massively against the interests of the less successful and, from then on, underprivileged sections of the population, its partisan activity can for a long time be expected to be met with tremendous tolerance even from those put to disadvantage, before it poses a threat to social harmony. The measures undertaken by the Bush administration and Congress to buy irrecoverable loans off the banks at zero cost and at the expense of the taxpayer, and to make funds available to banks in distress without demanding anything in return from these banks, only benefit the privileged section of the American population, though proving a burden on all taxpayers and increasing the share of public debt that falls to the lot of each and every citizen.[35]

The scope of action of American administrations is therefore considerably greater than that of the governments of continental Europe. This would have been of no further consequence if new constellations of power had not emerged under the impact of globalization, to the disadvantage of continental Europe.

11.7. The state in the hegemonic realm of power

No society can exist without the institutionalized power of the state, irrespective of the national, regional or global framework within which it acts. Hegemonic formations – globally operating transnational corporations and financial organizations – would, left to themselves, destroy their formless counterbalance in the long run, deform it in totalitarian fashion, obliterate the diversity of discourse essential to a vibrant democracy and reach no further understanding on the benchmarks and rules of coexistence. The downfall would then be unavoidable and even the most wonderful economic market theory would be unable to change anything. The present financial crisis serves as an overly clear example of this.[36]

State-level strategies of adjustment to the formless counterbalance of hegemonic formations that transcends national boundaries are operative even now in that law-enacting powers are passed on to international and regional authorities, and the sovereignty of the nation-state is, in increasing measure, subject to international law. Globalization is accompanied by the creation of new legal systems and a new dispensation of justice. In some cases, this development was directly supported by the nation-states; in other cases they were forced to accept that they were simply bypassed when these new forms were being shaped. Besides, national cultures, legal systems and approaches compete with each other for global implementation, this being particularly evident in trade law and international arbitration. In this area, the competition between the USA and Continental Europe does not remain at a level that is just moderate. The present financial crisis is considerable cause for conflict and may yet unleash major upheavals in the process of being tackled.

However, for elements of transnational legal cultures to evolve, an agreement on the principles of transnational justice is indispensable. Thus, for instance, the right to equal consideration constitutes the basic implementation of the principle of equality and manifests itself in the right to political participation. Such an interpretation of the principle of equality between nations accords validity to this political right of say at every institutional level at which political or economic decisions that tend to have a supranational impact are made. In keeping with the idea of co-determination, the basic rules of co-existence that fix mutual moral obligations must be agreed upon before corresponding mutual legal claims could emerge from their positivization. Such a process is hindered by the hegemonic claims of a power.

11.8. Conflict lines between the USA and hegemonic formations on the one side and Continental Europe on the other

The 14 measures conceived of by Germany's Social Democratic Party (SPD) to achieve greater transparency and stability in the financial markets are good pointers to the conflicts that may arise in negotiations between the states of Continental Europe and the USA. Although the individual points constitute maximum demands which would be scaled down during actual negotiation, some of the measures would have such deep implications for the financial structures that have evolved so far that the opposite side would reject them outright. The SPD calls for

- *greater liquidity and capital reserve requirements for financial institutions;*

The liquidity requirements set down by the supervision law must be expanded, liquidity risks factored in to a greater extent, liquidity margins established, stress tests optimized and supervision better incorporated. Similarly, there should be a marked increase in capital reserve requirements: we call for minimum capital ratios. This applies not least to credit extended to hedge funds for which at least 40% capital reserves should be set aside in future.

Even this at first glance seemingly plausible demand considerably curtails the banks' lending capacities and throws them open to state supervision, which is bound to be firmly rejected at the national level by the banks themselves and at the global level by the USA. Hedge funds in particular have so far been regarded by the banks as a welcome dividend-yielding instrument. Hedge funds could also be used to promote profitable deals which the banks themselves were not permitted to engage in. Up to now, the USA has staved off every attempt to infringe upon its sovereignty while at the same time remaining undeterred in its efforts to extend its hegemonic influence over other economies.

- *Stricter accounting as a mandatory requirement for financial institutions;*

In future, risks must be clearly identified on the balance sheets of financial institutions, without being passed on to special-purpose entities as has been the case so far. The EU Banking Directive is not sufficiently clear on this point. We believe it absolutely essential that risks be compulsorily represented on the basis of a standardized procedure. "Fair value measurement" as we know it today must be optimized against crises.

"Fair value measurement" [37] may be traced back to US accounting law. It supports the de-objectivization of corporate balance sheets. In this, the USA works in tandem with nationally and globally operating companies. The doctoring of balance sheets has been and still is an instrument of management for all financial institutions – an instrument they will dispense with only when subjected to the severest of pressure. The EU cannot exercise this requisite maximum pressure on its own. Holding companies maintained by transnational corporations and financial institutions in tax havens may also be classified as so-called special-purpose entities, established with the aim of escaping the dragnet of the national tax authorities.

- At least 20% retention on securitization;
We need greater risk awareness in the entire financial system. There should no longer be a separation between the decision to extend credit and the responsibility for the risk associated therewith. That is why financial institutions should no longer be permitted to securitize their credit risks 100% and pass them on. We are of the opinion that in future at least 20% of the risk should be borne by these institutions themselves on the basis of an international agreement.
This demand made by the SPD stands diametrically opposed to the practice prevalent in US investment and commercial banks. As already explained, US globalization policy is founded on the dissemination of infected credit demands across the globe. Any departure from this practice would have serious consequences for the hitherto US-dominated supply of liquid funds to the financial markets and will consequently be met with massive resistance from the USA and, to an extent, from the United Kingdom.

- A ban on harmful short sales;
Harmful 'short sales', that is to say, uncovered speculation on falling share prices have further aggravated the financial market crisis. Crisis-aggravating, harmful short sales must be banned at the international level.
The above formulation only refers to "crisis-aggravating" short sales. Short sales constitute a commonly used instrument on the stock exchange. They serve to explore market trends in the one or the other direction. Thus they inevitably carry a tinge of speculation. What the formulation does not address is the problem of how "crisis-aggravating" short sales should in the long run be distinguished from short sales that stabilize. To this extent, the demand for the ban on short sales will remain just a boldly demonstrative gesture that will fail to get implemented in the long run.

- Adjustment of the incentive and compensation schemes;
He who reaps the profits must also suffer the losses. In effecting changes in the incentive and compensation schemes in the financial sector on the basis of an

international 'code of behavior', we would like to ensure that in future errant behavior in individual cases will invite individual sanctions.

A manager gets a stake in the profits of his company or its rating on the stock exchange as a result of the shareholder principle. In course of time, top managers were no longer concerned whether they were adequately remunerated for their work; rather what interested them was where they stood in their ranking vis-à-vis their colleagues, both at home and abroad. A bonus system of this kind essentially knows no upper limit. The greater its hold over the day-to-day work of the concerned managers, the more damaging its impact on the long-term prospects of the entire corporate sector. At an average productivity growth rate of 2-3%, dividend demands of 20% and more can only be met in a real economy at the expense of wage earners and by pruning the welfare state. Further, if managers held personally liable for losses do not face any sanctions, the urge on the part of overly status-driven managers to feather their nests will become the driving force that actually propels their actions. A pre-requisite for the new code of behavior that the SPD seeks to introduce is that managers' salaries everywhere are fixed on the basis of the same criteria and subject to the same social values. But this is not the case, with the result that an understanding between the USA and Continental Europe hardly seems possible.

- *Personal liability for those responsible;*
The principle of 'privatizing profits and socializing losses' is unacceptable to us. We need international standards for assigning greater personal liability to financial market players. Their responsibility must also get reflected in the possibility for joint and individual liability.

Of particular relevance to this demand from the SPD is the difference in the social systems of the USA and Continental Europe. Richard von Weizsäcker, former president of Germany, once described the USA as a plutocracy in which approximately 200 well-off and well-established families are left to decide whether the Democratic or Republican Party is to be favored in the next legislative period. They accordingly extend financial and immaterial support to one of the two parties or presidential candidates in the fray. With regard to the socialization of losses and privatization of profits, these influential groups operating in a plutocratic society clearly decide in favor of the socialization of losses. Both the behavior of Congress and the Bush administration very clearly points to such a preference. In seeking to frame international standards, Continental Europe will be able to push through its demands only if the USA in the meantime touches an all-time economic low, and the majority of the American people withdraw their trust in the plutocrats.

- *European supervisory measures need to be strengthened;*
The European system of supervision needs to be further developed. Although initial steps have been taken, these are by no means adequate. Hence, the national and supranational cooperation of all supervisory authorities in

particular must ultimately be anchored in the EU Banking Directive. The next step would be to authorize the council of supervisory bodies involved in an international bank to take binding decisions.

On the face of it, this point does not appear to have any bearing on European-American relations. However, if there is no agreement here, the negotiating position of the Europeans vis-à-vis the Americans is bound to be severely compromised.

- Improved ratings;
The possibility of establishing a European rating agency as a counterweight to the agencies that had hitherto existed only in the USA must be examined. The advisory work of the rating agencies must be curtailed. Rating agencies must commit themselves to apply the IOSCO (Code of Conduct) which needs to be further developed. A European agency – possibly the Committee of European Security Regulators – should register and monitor rating agencies. The importance of ratings for risk assessment should be reduced.

As far as the three existing US rating agencies are concerned, the USA will presumably not concede joint European control. Rather, it will continue to publish the American agencies' ratings of companies and insist on these having binding force. It would then be up to the Europeans to accept or ignore them.

- A new, central role for the IMF;
We need enhanced early warning capacities and better cooperation between the IMF and the FSF. This apart, the core competences of both institutions must be combined and further developed upon. A joint annual report by the IMF and the FSF could enhance the effectiveness of crisis prevention in particular.

The FSF (Financial Stability Forum) was established in 1999 with the aim of achieving international financial stability through exchange of information and cooperation during financial inspection. The present financial crisis would not have occurred in the first place if information had been adequate and cooperation during inspection successful. How is one to achieve closer co-operation between the IMF and the FSF in negotiations with the US if the opposite side is not even willing to give up its vetoing minority in the IMF? As long as the USA does not distance itself from the borrowing option granted to it by Bretton Woods, only marginal success may be expected from cooperation between the IMF and the FSF.

- Hedge funds and private equity funds must be more effectively controlled and regulated;
Here, important keywords for us are: mandatory disclosure of the asset and ownership structure; greater obligation to provide information on the risks for investors; restriction of excessive external capital financing and restriction on investments.

On this issue, joint resistance may be expected from the USA and the transnational and globally active financial institutions. If we have two American hedge funds looking for long to destroy the "German Stock Exchange" in Frankfurt am Main with the intention of dealing a critical blow to a bothersome competitor to Wall Street and the City of London and, at the same time, do good business by selling the stocks of the German exchange, the motive we are up against is quite clear.

- *The demand for greater transparency in state investment funds;*

We welcome the most recent IMF-brokered progress in inducing state investment funds to commit themselves to greater transparency and support other European and bilateral steps towards the constructive incorporation of state investment funds into the global financial system.

Some state investment funds had reportedly been suspect, but obviously posed no threat, especially since they have in the meantime evolved into welcome investors that keep sick US banks afloat. Among such funds are the Abu Dhabi Investment Authority, United Arab Emirates; pension funds of the government of Norway; Government Investment Corp., Singapore; Central Bank of Saudi Arabia; Fund for Future Generations, Kuwait; Temasek, Singapore (the above funds have been listed on the basis of the size of the investment capital in billions of US dollars). When new names such as China Investment Corp and the Russian State Investment Fund joined the list, there was a sense of threat in the air, although they were until then not among the biggest international investors. The situation will have to be completely reassessed when the French state also establishes an investment fund in the future.

-*The participatory rights of workers should be strengthened;*

Co-determination in a company is an important instrument for the long-term existence of the company and must therefore be strengthened. There should be a clear tightening of sanctions for the violation of the mandatory requirements that a company furnish the works council with information – a requirement extended by the risk limitation act.

Co-determination is a particularly good example of the fundamental differences in perception regarding the role of the state. The above statements give no reason to expect that the long-term existence of companies in the USA will be made to depend on the existence of the works councils. There will be no agreements with the USA whatsoever in this area.

- *Tax havens must be drained dry;*

International tax havens and offshore financial centers, which are largely beyond the jurisdiction of laws and regulations, must be drained dry. Tax evasion in particular must be resolutely fought. To achieve this, it is necessary to seek out new paths. It is a matter of regret that tax havens and "havens for parking black money" still exist in Europe. That is why Europe must also *proceed to take further action to check them. It is with this in mind that we call for the EU-Interest and Royalties Directive to be revised.*

As long as EU members such as the United Kingdom (Canary Islands, Isle of Man, Gibraltar), Luxemburg, Austria, France (Monaco, Andorra), Spain (Andorra) and Italy (San Marino) in Europe benefit from the presence of tax havens, every attempt to drain out the non-European tax havens will remain futile. The UK in particular maintains tax havens in other parts of the world, as do France and the Netherlands, and the USA backs some of them to a considerable extent.

- *Germany's Three-Pillar Model should be retained – regional banks consolidated;*

The project group supports the three-tiered German banking system with its highly decentralized structures consisting of savings banks, cooperative banks and commercial banks. The composite structures of the savings banks and commercial banks have proved their stabilizing impact particularly in the present crisis. This is one of the reasons why we reject the idea of converting savings banks into joint-stock companies and other organizations under private law. Public-sector regional banks must be horizontally consolidated.

Agreements with the USA are ruled out even in this area since a banking structure of this kind is totally unknown in the USA. Other detailed demands made by the SPD under these 14 points have not been presented here.

11.9. The competitive advantage that the US bailout is intended to achieve

„In a number of ways, the American bailout is being given fewer strings than are bailouts in European countries. While that would seem to place the American government at a disadvantage, it could rebound to its benefit if that relative leniency helps the banks to recover quickly and provides the government with a big profit on the equity stake it is receiving. Whereas some of the European plans barred banks from paying dividends on common stock until the government got its money back, and demanded promises that the banks would keep loans flowing to businesses and individuals, the U.S. government said that the banks it invested in could continue to pay dividends on existing common and preferred shares. In addition, while European banks are being required in some cases to put government representatives on their boards of directors, the American government will not receive board representation or have voting power." (Floyd Norris, ibid.).

In summing up, Norris puts forth the view that the USA should play for time so that it could regain its hegemonic position at the next opportune moment. The measures taken by the Bush administration and the Federal Reserve would only subject the financial industry to controls of an extremely mild nature, with the result that it can recover from the crisis far more quickly than its European counterpart. If Plan B were to actually be implemented in the USA, the European governments would find themselves at a crucial turning point: Would they be ready to assert themselves as equal partners of the USA or would they allow themselves to be split once again, with every government trying its luck at negotiating on its own? The USA would ultimately emerge the winner and, after an effective interval of time, once again hold up the „Follow me!" sign to the Europeans.

James K. Galbraith expresses this in somewhat friendlier terms in his article 'The Global Financial Crisis – and what the new US President should do' (Die Weltfinanzkrise – und was der neue US-Präsident tun sollte), Blätter für deutsche und internationale Politik, Issue 11, 2008, p. 57): ‚The new President must prepare himself to explain that the real objective of the United States is to assume the leadership role in a global community, that is to say, the task of heading collective action on a large scale.' („Der neue Präsident sollte sich darauf einstellen zu erklären, dass die Führungsrolle in einer Weltgemeinschaft – die Aufgabe, kollektives Handeln im großen Maßstab anzuführen – die wahre Bestimmung der Vereinigten Staaten ist."). Even he dreams of the USA regaining its „role as technology leader", now that it has forfeited its „financial hegemonial role". But in the aftermath of the Bush era, there will presumably be no going back to the status of a „well-meaning hegemony" which the US had enjoyed in earlier decades.

12. Conclusions

12.1. The transience of empires and hegemonies

Power constellations have emerged in all periods of human coexistence, but entities as complex as hegemonies or empires have only materialized at higher levels of development. Domination was founded for the most part on the rule of the fittest, bestowed by God himself upon the worthiest, or wielded through representation of the people. Even though all forms of rule were transient in nature, they often bore the aura of immortality. The epithet „holy" for instance (the term hierarchy = holy order denotes nothing but this) was meant to bestow greater sanctification upon the very earthen systems of temporal rule.

The history of development of types of rule and the specific accumulation of power associated therewith has by no means been linear. Periods dominated by forms of rule characterized by the rapid accumulation of power were followed by others in which rule was associated more with the renunciation and decline of power. Simultaneously occurring developments – both parallel and contrary – in the evolution of forms of rule did not permit the exploration of a general line of development, although advancing technology as a universal constant has remained a factor that influences the acquisition and maintenance of power, and the shaping of new forms of rule. Even though in the past, empires and hegemonies had at times extended across the globe, and even though the sun never set on them, there were in and beside them undominated - though disputed - territories which could be exploited by their rivals for the deployment of their own power. With the end of the 'East-West' conflict in 1990, an entirely new constellation seemed to take shape for the first time in the history of mankind. This was regarded by the power elite in the USA as a useful challenge to lend its – until then territorially restricted – hegemony a global dimension.

12.2. Reasons for the rise and fall of Pax Americana

12.2.1. The phenomenal rise of the USA

The multicultural community that came to settle on the North American continent had left behind the „old world", determined not only to take on the European colonial regimes in the „New World" but to also found something essentially new in society. This community of settlers found fertile land available on an expanse of settled territory. The subjugation of the indigenous Indian population, which commenced at this time, and the exploitation of the African slaves did not restrict the „white man's" creative force and capacity, nor did it stir his conscience. Rather, it was interpreted by him as a sign of divine intervention to help the „good" and the „progressive" achieve a breakthrough over the backward peoples on the entire American continent. Spurred by the self-emasculation of the European countries from where the settlers originally hailed, and favored by the early adoption of industrial mass production, the USA succeeded in establishing itself as an effective rival to the old industrial nations of Europe by the beginning of the 20th century itself. As a result, by the end of World War I, the USA had emerged as a deft, calculating capital provider to the divided, financially drained European states which had come to lag behind the US economically. After the Second World War, the USA actually came close to achieving its goal of overcoming the confining isolation of the American continent from the European and Asian markets – an isolation wrought by oceans on either side – thereby establishing itself as a preeminent power both in Western Europe and the coastal regions of the Pacific. The emerging conflict with the economically weaker Soviet Union was used by the US to gather together its own economic and military strength and steadily enhance it, so that with the added advantage of its own cultural appeal, it could not only consolidate its position of supremacy in the coastal regions of the Atlantic and Pacific but also emerge victorious in the East-West conflict.[38]

12.2.2. Hypertrophic hegemonial consciousness

After being locked in a dual hegemony with the USA for a period of forty years, the Soviet Union lost its status as a hegemonic power. As the sole remaining hegemon, the USA took up the challenge of assuming exclusive control and extended its sway both over the territory controlled by its partner/adversary until then, as well as over the non-aligned regions between the two camps. A period of indefinite American control over the rest of the world, in which there would be no more scope for potential rivals to emerge, would characterize the end of history from the perspective of the US elites (Francis Fukuyama).

Accordingly, the discussion on the difference between empire and hegemony had, for instance, lost all meaning for the American leadership. For the latter, America's welfare had become synonymous with the welfare of the entire global community. This mindset was mirrored in the unilateral behavior of the American leadership. Likewise, differentiating between *willing* and *unwilling* „partners", branding the ostracized as „*rogues*" and reducing uprisings with the most varied of histories to condemnable acts of „*international terrorism*" was the result of the very same mindset. In fact, convinced they were all-powerful, US administrations even perceived the globalization of the markets, propagated and furthered by them to support the global activities of transnational corporations and financial capital, as proof of their growing power. Thus, with the focus of US attention being primarily directed outward and with its sights set on the expansion of its hegemony, the demands of the country's long-neglected infrastructure and its uncompetitive, obsolete industries were completely overlooked. The growing disorientation of influential US elites was evidenced in the undue emphasis they gave to their international standing and in the decline they suffered within their own ranks. They overlooked or ignored the real challenges approaching them.

12.2.3. Rising intra-societal tensions
During the second term of the Bush administration, the USA for the first time in its history was to witness both the strengthening of its economic competitors and incipient signs of social and economic weakness within the country. Several members of the now rich American upper middle class had begun to relocate or, rather, allowed sizable sections of the industrial and service sectors under their control to relocate to lower-cost shores abroad (that is, to the so-called emerging economies). They also started investing the income from the relocation of production in lucrative financial schemes, while drastic cuts pushed through in Congress during the terms of President Clinton and President Bush ensured that there was an expected increase in net incomes given the sharp rise in gross incomes.

Under the impact of this relocation, the middle class on the other hand had to come to terms with just marginally rising or even stagnating wages and salaries, though initially it was kept happy with low-priced imports from the emerging economies. Further, it was also lured into believing that its houses, purchased with loans, would have higher resale value, and deluded about its steady progressive decline through generous offers of consumer credit. As for the already impoverished lower class with its low level of education, it was to see an ever-increasing number of welfare benefits withdrawn by the state. The latter also drove those dependent on ill-paid, part-time jobs, and those left to helplessly cope with the consequences of disease on their own without insurance cover, deeper into the vortex of poverty and deprivation.

The deepening divide between the „moneyed elite" at the apex of the social pyramid, the status-driven middle class – wedged between this elite and the lower class – and the increasingly impoverished lower class resulted in the erosion of social cohesion and harmony in American society. Of course it was not the principle of equality but happiness and individual efforts for success that were set down as the basic ingredients for social cohesion when American society was first founded. Even so, the unbridled self-enrichment of the rich and the top income group in US society was to increasingly violate the basic, long-standing consensus in American settler society, creating in it considerable tensions which for the first time were accompanied by symptoms of hegemonic overreach.

12.2.4. Indications of US-hegemonic overreach
The USA's hegemonic position remained undisputed as long as it restricted itself to dominating the intra-Western triangle of USA-Japan-Western Europe, while leveraging the side-benefits emanating from the East-West conflict. By and large, towards Western Europe and Japan, the USA favored a benevolent hegemony whereas in its relations with Latin America and the oil-producing countries of the Middle East, it displayed a negative side that was purely power-oriented and interventionist.

It was only after the dissolution of its co-hegemon, the USSR, at the beginning of the 90s – a development it had encouraged without realizing that its own hegemonic ambitions could also be shattered in the bargain – that the USA got itself ensnarled in the uncertain terrain of globalization. The fall of the Soviet Union meant that the Pacific-rim states and those on the West-European fringes of the East-West conflict, which had earlier been hegemonized within the intra-Western triangle, no longer felt the pressure of the East-West conflict bearing down upon them, this also being true of the Latin Americans who were more or less being treated as servitors. The latter on their part pushed for equal treatment and rejected the continuation of American hegemony, which was now thrust upon them by way of the American demand that these countries adopt the – apparently – extremely successful American economic and social system. From the viewpoint of the future global hegemon, all hegemonized economies had to function on the lines of the American model and orient themselves to the prime trading and financial centers of New York and London. Resistance from continental Europe to the Anglo-American model was sparked off particularly by the American demand that, in deference to neo-liberalism, the European states abdicate the welfare-state systems on which the maintenance of social harmony within their societies rested. The only way to break their resistance would be if the American globalization strategy were to expand to the so-called emerging economies (such as China, India, Mexico etc.), and if transnational corporations engaged there used their low production costs to apply pressure on the established, highly industrialized economies.

American companies and financial organizations, which had somewhat recklessly maintained at the start that they could flood the Chinese market with American goods and, by way of exchange, sell cheap Chinese products on the American market, were soon to be taught a lesson. For, it was not the USA which would make its presence felt on the Chinese market but, on the contrary, China which would flood the US market with a growing tide of goods produced in Chinese factories. The reason for this was that the relocation of production centers from the USA to China not only suited the heads of American companies who raked in additional profits as a result, but could for a long time also keep American consumers in the dark about the long-term impacts of production relocations by supplying them with low-cost consumer goods produced in China. In giving precedence to their personal interest in profit over the social consensus on the primacy of the welfare of the American nation (valid until then for all sections of US citizenry), those members of US society who were single-minded in their pursuit of ever more wealth, succeeded in undermining the USA's position of supremacy in a globalized world. They also undermined social cohesion in the US in a manner similar to what had occurred in the feudal states of Old Europe where feudal lords had hastened to emulate the rising bourgeoisie, and entrepreneurs sought to become rich and influential. These feudal lords-turned-capitalist entrepreneurs destroyed the consensus on preserving the social basis of feudalism prevalent until then across all ranks of nobility, undermined the privileges of the nobility and strengthened the bourgeoisie which had been demanding equal rights for all members of society. However, the USA's globalization ambitions were ultimately thwarted by China's unwillingness to become part of the extended intra-Western triangle of USA, Western Europe and Japan. Although China opened its doors to investment capital flowing in from transnational corporations, Chinese leadership at no point of time let the reins of the state slip out of its hands. To this extent its behavior and approach differed dramatically from that of the Russian leadership under President Yeltsin. The USA also did not succeed in palming off co-hegemony to the Chinese leaders. It even lost the considerable influence it had wielded on Putin's Russia and, in the case of India, was forced to ultimately accept the fact that despite signing the nuclear deal with it, the much-wooed India would not engage in quid pro quo by containing China. On the contrary, the leading Asian countries – China, Russia and India – forged closer ties with each other, and even Japan and South Korea were moving closer to this overarching political and economic cooperation in Asia. Besides, with the exception of Great Britain, the other West European powers also seemed open to the establishment of a common Eurasian economic zone. However, they still had to convince the East European members of the European Union of the benefits of such a partnership. For, these East European countries, particularly Poland and the Czech Republic, still considered the USA their protector. It was only when the USA failed to intervene militarily in the conflict between Georgia and Russia that these East European countries seemed to realize that they could not rely on the USA.

12.2.5. The financial crisis as a portent for the USA's unavoidable adjustment to the multilateral structure

The USA's credibility has taken a severe beating due to the setbacks it has suffered in the two wars waged by it in Iraq and Afghanistan. Its reputation with the international public has suffered even more on account of it permitting torture in the so-called „war on terror". But it was the financial crisis emanating from the USA that destroyed the basic confidence the country had until then commanded as the leading financial power. The final blow was dealt by the former head of the Nasdaq stock exchange, Bernard L. Madoff, who in the biggest Wall Street scam to date relieved his creditors of over 50 billion US dollars. The USA will cease to serve as a secure destination for monetary investments in future; the dollar will forfeit its position as the world's reserve currency; as in the case of all other countries, US trade deficits too will have to be managed through austerity measures.

With that, the USA would lose its hegemonic standing as a financial power. It would have to join the concert of leading global powers as one among them and see itself compelled to modernize its own economy in response to a pressing demand. A new version of the „New Deal" is already being planned under the newly elected American President, Obama. In all probability, plans to modernize a dilapidated infrastructure, the domestic industry and the service sector can only be financed through a drastic reduction in military expenditure. As a result, the USA would lose its capacity to maintain a military presence across the world and to intervene in conflicts in some form or the other. With that, it would also have forfeited its military status as a hegemonic power. The USA would consequently suffer the same fate as many hegemonic powers that have failed before it. In the majority of the cases, it was the influential political elites of these powers that ushered in their decline by putting their own interests before those of society at large. In concert with other intra-societal forces, they either accepted the overweening nature of their hegemony, often linked to their supreme interests, or did not recognize the threat posed by it early enough.

Even before he assumed office in January 2009 as the newly elected President of the United States, Obama's recommendations for change and renewal within the US had met with considerable resistance in Congress. The conflict between a work-generating employment programme on the one hand and a consumer-friendly general reduction in taxes on the other has served to divide the Democrats and the Republicans in both Houses of Congress. It is highly doubtful whether the much-needed reform of the health-care system will be supported by a majority from both the Senate and the House of Representatives this time after futile attempts in the past. Likewise, given the competition for military supply contracts between the individual states of the Union, and the prestige that goes with securing the same, it is not yet clear what the scale of resistance would be to cuts in military expenditure. The Federal Reserve interest rate, reduced to almost zero to overcome economic recession, and the almost unlimited increase in US dollars, will only lead to a drastic devaluation of the US currency. It is not yet clear how the owners of US treasury bonds will react thereto. One of the likely fallouts could be a flight to the euro.

Hegemonic consciousness persists for a long time, as the still prevailing mindset of Russia's power elite amply illustrates. Needless to say, it would virtually demand superhuman effort on the part of the prominent US elite to not only tone down but altogether abandon its leadership-driven thinking and behavior and take its place in the concert of global powers as an equal among equals. Efforts on the part of the Europeans and, in particular, efforts of the so-called Transatlantic group to establish a relationship of parity between Europe and the USA could come to nought due to rigid patterns of thinking in the USA and subservient behavior - in part unconscious - prevalent on the other side.

13. Afterword

13.1. The present situation of departure – Threat of inflation as the basic problem

The Czech Prime Minister, Mirek Topolanek, called US President Barack Obama's crisis management policy the „road to hell" (t-online.de, 25.3.2009). The stimulus packages, he believed, would even undermine the stability of the global financial markets. In order to finance its economic relief measures, the US would have to bring government bonds to the market, for which there would however be no buyers at present.[39] There are two questions that need to be answered: When does the threat of inflation arise and how can inflationary developments be stemmed in time?

In reality, the US Central Bank (FED) felt compelled to buy up government bonds. For if there are no – or merely insufficient – purchase orders from private buyers, the state does indeed receive „fresh funds" to the tune of the amount paid by the Central Bank for the bonds, though this amount is not balanced by a corresponding reduction in the quantum of money in the non-state sector. Over the period of validity of government bonds, there is an increase in the total quantity of US dollars in circulation – in other words, there is an increase in inflation potential. It is only later, when the state seeks to redeem its bonds from the central bank and deposits the corresponding value in cash, that it once again curtails the inflation potential that had opened up.

Topolanek's criticism is unjustified in periods of crisis during which inter-bank transactions come to a halt. If banks do not extend loans to each other for lack of trust, there will be a drastic fall in the amount of money circulating in the financial market. The state will then step in by infusing „fresh money" into the market.

But on the other hand, if there is greater trust between the banks, and interbank trading once again reaches a scale commensurate with the real economy, then the additional quantum of money pumped in by the government and the Central Bank could well pave the way for an inflationary development. For, as long as the state does not redeem its bonds from the central bank, instead increasing its budget deficit further, and as long as the central bank does not find any buyers for the government bonds in its custody, there will be a sharp increase in the inflation potential.

Thus in order to prevent such a development, those states engaged in addressing the prevailing financial crisis should by then have ensured that the global financial operations of the banks, hedge funds, private equity firms and pension funds are more tightly regulated. If not, we face the prospect of the next bubble emerging and bringing with it consequences that are even more devastating.

13.2. US global strategy as the cause for the present financial crisis

The European states, Japan and some emerging economies must finally put an end to their unquestioning adoption of the American globalization strategy, conceived during President Bill Clinton's first term itself and duly implemented with the first set of measures adopted. These states to an extent submitted to this strategy despite being fully aware of the repercussions it could have for other models of society.

When in the autumn of 1998 the German Federal Chancellor Gerhard Schröder admitted that he would not engage in „politics that went against the economy", he voiced a certain distance from the demands made in the USA, though there was no counterstrategy detectable in his words. Other than some words of reassurance, Schröder had no response to the dictum of the Chairman of the Deutsche Bank, Josef Breuer, who remarked: "The structure of the international financial markets reflects the community of values of the Western world", or to the former President of the Bundesbank, Tietmeyer, when he pronounced: "Gentlemen, you are now under the control of the financial markets" (From Oskar Lafontaine's introduction to Heiner Flassbeck's book entitled „Gescheitert", in: „Das Casino schließen - der Ökonom Heiner Flassbeck zur globalen Finanzkrise" by Frank Hahn, Solon-line, 25 March 2009).

Even Federal Finance Minister Steinbrück's pronouncement that the German Federal Government had over the turn of the century been "open" to market liberalization and the innovation of financial products for fear of not being able to retain Frankfurt am Main as a financial center, is indicative of a strategy of adjustment but not the unfolding of a counterstrategy (Peer Steinbrück, Warum die Krise eine Zäsur ist, *Die Zeit*, 26. 4. 2009).[40]

British governments had been entirely preoccupied with shoring up the financial center of London. As long as the City of London raked in sufficient tax revenue for the Labour Government to finance its social welfare programs, it held on firmly to its special status with the USA and adopted every measure – sensible or not – that found its way across the Atlantic.

Japan, China and India were thankful for the inflated financial markets and the USA's policy of indebtedness. Without an American policy of this kind, the export prospects for the services and manufactures of these countries would have recorded much slower growth.

At present, the entire group of established industrialized countries, the industrially emerging countries and the still industrially backward Third World countries in particular are faced with the far-reaching consequences of their subservience to the American globalization strategy. As of now, it is not even sure whether the stabilization of the financial markets can be ensured.

13.3. Closure of the global financial casino as a crisis management strategy for the present financial and economic crisis

13.3.1. Measures for the short-term stabilization of the financial markets

A series of bad tidings forced the states to intervene. Thus, Merrill Lynch's takeover by Bank of America proved to be a bottomless 'debt-pit', and finally cost the head of Bank of America his post. The large American mortgage banks Freddy Mac and Fanny Mae, which dominate the American mortgage market, urgently needed billions of dollars more from the state in order to survive. American International Group (AIG), that insurance giant with a worldwide presence, had to be rescued from total collapse by the state, because a collapse would have meant immeasurable damage to the global financial market. An ever-increasing number of private equity funds showed themselves to be no longer capable of closing the crucial circle of „rais(ing) money, invest(ing) it, add(ing) (a) lashing of debt, dress(ing) up the portfolio of companies and sell(ing) them at a profit". „The number of private equity firms that completed fund-raising efforts in the first quarter fell by more than 70 percent from the first quarter of last year." (Lauren Silva Laughlin, Buyout fund investors now in the driver's seat, *International Herald Tribune*, April 15, 2009). Other British banks passed into state hands. The banks of Iceland were all nationalized, the customers of the UBS Bank of Switzerland withdrew billions from the bank, and in the wake of losses that ran into billions, the bank announced that 8700 jobs would be axed (*Frankfurter Rundschau*, 15.4.2009). Belgium's Fortis Bank suffered a loss of 20.6 billion euros in 2008 (*Tagesspiegel*, 15.4.2009). American life insurers were not only confronted with sizable losses in the value of the mortgage instruments in their possession but also had to contend with an increasing number of non-payments on the part of companies which were on the verge of bankruptcy. The next debacle that loomed on the horizon in April 2006 was the threat of some of the largest American credit card companies – Mastercard, Visa, American Express, Capital One, HSBC, Citigroup, Wells Fargo and Bank of America – collapsing.

Although – as per the International Monetary Fund (IMF) – the combined losses of the global financial economy have in the meantime risen to 4 trillion US dollars, and bank balance sheets reportedly contain a sizable number of other bad holdings whose disposal is still a matter of contention (*Tagesspiegel*, 20.4./22.4.2009), bank managers have invariably refused to forego the bonuses assured them in better times, thereby evoking angry reactions from people across the world. There was even more anger when US banks made the transparent attempt to show profits once again on the basis of changes in accounting rules, and leveraged the apparent success to evade the American government's stress tests to determine the banks' capital base as well as to bypass state supervision on the whole. It must be noted that as per preliminary reports, around 50% of the large American banks need to raise fresh capital again to overcome the financial crisis (*Frankfurter Rundschau*, 6.5.2009).

According to the Wall Street Journal, Bank of America alone obviously has an additional financial requirement of 35 billion US dollars, and as per a report in the New York Times, the Citigroup needs 5 to 10 billion and Wells Fargo 15 billion (*Tagesspiegel*, 7.5.2009).
Despite the devastating outcome of the neo-liberal policy of deregulation, bankers continue to be sceptical about the wisdom of the new regulations. „The biggest issue for banks – and indeed insurance companies – is whether the accounting rules are sensible", commented Charlie McCreevy, European Commissioner for the Internal Market and Services, in an interview with Karina Robinson (*International Herald Tribune*, April, 11-12, 2009). But Martin Hellwig believes that despite many bank managers being understandably averse to being toppled by the state, it is inevitable that the system of bank regulation will get "completely" overhauled in the long run (Interview with Robert Heusinger „Dieses System ist katastrophal", *Frankfurter Rundschau*, 7. 4. 2009). What form it could then assume has already been the subject of discussions at the G-20 Summit in London in the beginning of April 2009.

13.3.2. The long-term reform of the economic and financial system
The Continent's fears that the USA and Great Britain would only push for massive stimulus packages at the G-20 London Summit, thereby neglecting the as-yet-unaddressed regulation of the financial markets, proved to be unfounded. Once it became clear to the Anglo-American representatives, even before the start of the Conference, that the countries of the euro area could introduce far-reaching regulatory measures even without the consent of the United Kingdom and the United States, they gave up the idea of a confrontation. US representatives in particular had to admit that the enormous imbalance between the US-share of the world's gross national product (amounting to 1/5) and US-share of currency reserves held by all central banks (about 75%) calls for urgent redressal. Chinese representatives made sure they were not overheard when they called for the US dollar – the only currency to be recognized by the International Monetary Fund as the world reserve currency – to be replaced by a basket of currencies or a world reserve currency backed and guaranteed by a group of countries. Even before the IMF could adopt corresponding resolutions in the months to follow, the representatives of G-20 gathered in London stripped the IMF of the function it had hitherto exercised as the merely extended arm of the USA's global political strategy. Instead, it was to once again contribute decisively to the risk-bearing capacity of the entire global financial system in particular. On the 23rd of April 2009, the head of the IMF, Dominique Strauss-Kahn, for the first time even spoke out in favor of canceling the USA's right of veto (*Focus Magazin Finanzen*, 24.4.2009).
At the same time, the screws were also tightened on tax havens. Those that were willing to cooperate found themselves on a grey list (as for instance, the Cayman Islands, Liechtenstein, Austria, Belgium, Chile, Monaco, the Netherlands, Luxemburg, Singapore, Switzerland) and those unwilling to cooperate for the

time being were placed on a black list (Costa Rica, Malaysia, Philippines, Uruguay). Although the USA found itself on the white list of "willing states", the future tax-concealing role of the individual federal states in the US (such as Delaware) went unmentioned.

The Conference ended with a vague rejection of protectionism (that crisis-aggravating outcome of the global economic crisis of 1929/34) and the promise to prevent competitive cycles of devaluation. All regulatory loopholes on the financial market were to be plugged. The Financial Stability Board (FSB), the international supervisory body, was to be strengthened, though only the important hedge funds were to be brought under control. Further, it is still entirely unclear whether it would be this body or another that would be equipped to push through an anti-cyclical regulatory policy. Which of the states would then be willing to give up a part of their – until then – ostensibly independent monetary and financial policy for the sake of this body.

Following the G-20 Conference, the World Bank put together an investment package running into billions for the less industrialized countries, which were still not in a position to finance their own relief programs. Besides, various models were discussed for the establishment of so-called bad banks, through which banks could dispose of their problematic bonds (Stephan Kaiser, Regierung einigt sich auf Bad Banks, *Tagesspiegel*, 22.4.2009). The Swedish example, cited at length in the interview with Martin Hellwig, would require that all banks be first nationalized or placed under state control and then categorized into "good" and "bad" banks. The "bad" bank would remain under state control and the "good" bank privatized. The "bad" bank would retain the dubious instruments and be liquidated in due course. The "good" bank would receive the good assets as well as the customers' deposits, apart from sufficient capital of its own from the taxpayer. The profits of the "good" bank would also enhance the common stock of the "good" bank, which would be held by the "bad" bank. In the event of the ultimately unavoidable collapse of the "bad" bank, the taxpayer would benefit from the profits of the "good" bank while the expropriated original shareholders would emerge from the situation with nothing. If, ultimately, the "bad" bank is rendered solvent, then the original shareholders would also stand to benefit (ibid.)

Heiner Flassbeck proposed the following measures for globally addressing the financial crisis: "It is technically simple to remove the toxic assets from the balance sheets of the banks. We must ideally set up an international clearing house through which these toxic holdings are liquidated, so that the banks could once again devote themselves to their core business of lending" (ibid.). No one knows as yet how long it will take for the credit markets to start functioning again. Meanwhile, what appears to be far more pressing is the need to boost the real economy, which has been hit by the financial crisis and is even on the verge of collapse in some places.

In the leading industrial countries, the gross domestic product has already shrunk by 6% in the last decade of 2008 and the first quarter of 2009. The decline in economic growth is more rapid in the present global economic crisis than during the World Economic Crisis of 1929 (Thomas Fischermann, „Schneller – aber auch tiefer?, *Die Zeit*, 16. 4. 2009). Economic researchers differ on how the economic development of the near future is to be represented: as a horizontally extended U-form or an elongated L-form with little prospect of stimulation. No longer does anyone dream of a sharp turn-around following a steep descent, or for that matter of the hoped-for and just-as-sharp ascent.

Corporate loans may now be secured on stock exchanges at increasingly favorable rates. Insolvency administrators are in great demand both with companies and states. Increasingly, the BRIC states – Brazil, Russia, India and China – fail to serve as buffers for the old industrial world. The calling-in of loans extended in the past to less developed countries in the Third World and to the East European countries results in the latter's economies plunging, while at the same time, surplus-funds countries, while purchasing land, increasingly invest their foreign exchange in inflation-secure Third World countries (Marie-Béatrice Baudet et Laetitia Clavreul, Les terres agricoles, de plus en plus convoitées, *Le Monde*, 15 April 2009). Mass unemployment continues to spread. The costs of salvaging the banking sector in the US and elsewhere, and of stimulating the economy (for instance the automobile industry), are rising astronomically although it is not sure whether the targeted goals will actually be achieved. The USA will spearhead efforts to drain out tax havens (Reuters, SNAP ANALYSIS - Obama takes first step in tax overhaul, May 4, 2009). The new European System of Financial Supervision is meant to be in place by 2010 as per the schedule of the European Commission; however, conservative forecasts indicate that it can only be expected to be operational in 2011 when the crisis in the real economy comes to an end.

But what continues to boom regardless of the economic downturn is arms production and the trade in arms. Sipri puts the USA (with 34.9 billion $) and Russia (with 28.5 billion) down to be the world's largest and second largest exporters of arms between 2004 and 2008. They are followed by Germany (11.5 billion $) and other European countries (*Frankfurter Rundschau*, 28.4.09). The largest importers of arms in the period 2004-2008 are China (13 billion), India (8.2 billion), UAE (7.1 billion), South Korea (6.9 billion), Greece (4.8 billion) and Israel (4.6 billion). Along the lines of conflict that run between some of these countries and their adversaries, there could possibly be war breaking out in the future. And it is for successfully waging such wars that measures will be taken today for employment generation programs that will primarily serve to arm these countries.

13.4. A historical perspective – Alternative strategies for overcoming global economic crises

Examples both of success and failure drawn from the history of the 20th century reveal the alternative measures which the states had resorted to in order to contain the harmful effects of the financial crises created by the bursting of credit bubbles. Such crisis management measures include the stimulation of the armament industry in war preparation strategies, the credit-financed renewal of the infrastructure and/or the state-supported development of new technologies as well as the comprehensive restructuring of relations between state and society. Reactions, for instance from the USA and Germany, to the world economic recession of 1929 differed greatly.

13.4.1. The New Deal in the USA

After the 14th of October 1929, the mood on the New York Stock Exchange had turned. There was a surge in the sale of bonds. By 29th October 1929, the sale had reached panic proportions. Hoover, Roosevelt's Republican predecessor, had adopted a policy of lowering taxes and interest as a way of countering the economic and financial crisis. However, this policy proved a failure as did the re-linking of currencies to gold (not just in the USA).

There was no program elaborate in content that was at the core of Roosevelt's New Deal. Under pressure to achieve results in the short term, the democratically constituted Congress adopted a series of laws on state intervention in the financial and economic sectors during a "100-day" emergency session shortly after Roosevelt assumed office on 4th March 1933. These laws involved for instance the regulation of the finance sector, employment generation programs, social welfare measures, promotion of economic development, regulation of agriculture, regional development, state support for house owners faced with the threat of foreclosure sales, and the removal of the gold standard.[41]

Among the achievements of the New Deal were, firstly, preventing panic in the banking sector as well as the subsequent collapse of the entire financial system in the spring of 1933 and, secondly, effecting a slowdown in the spread of mass unemployment, which until the winter of 1933-34 had grown by leaps and bounds. In 1934, the USA's gross domestic product was 15% higher than that of 1933, yet 15% below the 1932 level (Michael Liebig, „War on the Depression" - Der Erste New Deal (1933-34) und sein Vorläufer: die War Mobilization (1917-18). „The New Deal mobilization of 1933-34, from which so much had been expected, brought disappointing economic returns", commented Braeman/ Leuchtenburg (Braeman, John (ed.): Change and Continuity in 20th Century America, New York, 1964; see therein: *Leuchtenburg, William: The New Deal and the Analogy of War*, p. 127).

Since war mobilization measures of 1917-18 had served as a model for the first New Deal, these beginnings could be harked back to once again when the new version of the New Deal was launched. The second New Deal served to prepare the USA for entry into the Second World War. Thus, measures adopted in the US began to be more in tune with crisis management strategies, which elsewhere had been pursued on a priority basis much earlier.

13.4.2. Crisis management through arms build-up in Germany

Industrial production declined by 50% in Germany. With a view to balancing the trade deficit and boosting the export economy, the government under Reichskanzler Heinrich Brüning reacted with emergency decrees for curtailing public expenditure, pruning the salaries of civil servants, increasing taxes, social spending and duties, and for decreasing wages by up to 50%. Every third member of the workforce lost his job. In 1933, there were 6 million unemployed, while 23.3 million Germans lived on unemployment and social welfare benefits. With the drastic re-distribution of wage-based income to income from entrepreneurial activity – a re-distribution linked to these measures – there was a surge of public disenchantment with democracy, while radical parties gained vigorous support and social unrest spread.

The National Socialist Party of Germany (NSDAP) led by Adolf Hitler, which had grown in strength after the Reichstag elections, not only benefited from the rigorous measures adopted by the Brüning government but itself launched an employment-generating rearmament program immediately on coming to power. This certainly served to reduce mass unemployment, but at the same time also prepared the way for participation in the Second World War. The "New Deal", launched by the National Socialists to overcome the global economic crisis was arms-oriented from the very start, hailed by the German heavy industry and backed by the leading banks as well.

13.5. Conclusions

Both before and after the World Economic Crisis of 1929, states for the most part proceeded in a manner driven by protectionism, a pro-cyclical fiscal and budgetary policy, narrow nationalism dogged claims to hegemonial positions, revanchism and fear of social unrest. History, to be sure, does not repeat itself in the same form, yet similar constellations could well evoke similar responses. Strategies evolved so far for overcoming the financial and economic crisis point in a different direction. However, once the USA and Europe are confronted with the question as to whether the Anglo-American or the continental form of capitalism or – globally speaking – the Chinese has greater resilient strength, there is the danger of individual camps emerging and military aspects once again being accorded greater importance. In such a scenario, rearmament worldwide will be an easy way of responding to heightened fears and, at the same time, will also be lauded as a still available and so far insufficiently deployed means of overcoming the crisis.

14. Notes and References

1. Following the withdrawal of the French in 1955, South Vietnam increasingly turned to the USA, with North Vietnam thereupon leaning more towards the Soviet Union. This only served to further aggravate the historically precarious relationship between the Vietnamese and China (given that Vietnam had in former times either partly belonged to China or come under strong Chinese influence, or even been occupied by Chinese troops). The greater the success gained by North Vietnam in overcoming the partition of the country by infiltrating the South, the lesser China's interest in continuing to allow Soviet arms supplies to pass through Chinese territory en route to North Vietnam (initially Chinese interest was largely confined to lifting military technology to upgrade the inferior military goods that the Soviets supplied to China - as against India - or to replace them with indigenous production).
At the same time, the Chinese leadership sought to demonstrate to the US that it could not win guerrilla wars merely with state-of-the-art weaponry. From the Chinese strategic perspective, Vietnam should ideally remain partitioned, though US influence on South Vietnam should wane and be replaced by Chinese influence. China temporarily confined itself to the neutralization of South Vietnam but, ultimately, even back then, it regarded the entire South China Sea as being part of the Chinese zone of influence.

2. By participating, Great Britain and France signaled that they considered their – in the meantime – high degree of dependence on the USA (Suez Canal reversal, 1956) less serious than the possible unification of Germany.
The US administration did not intervene decisively during the East German revolt of 1953 and the Hungarian uprising of 1956. Against the backdrop of Anglo-French attempts to preserve their influence in the Eastern part of the Mediterranean (with the Suez Canal conflict raging at the same time), the USA and the Soviet Union helped each other stabilize their hegemonic power in Europe at the expense of their European allies in each case. The self-assertion of the USA and the Soviet Union as hegemonies or the assertion of their claim to being hegemonies vis-à-vis the Europeans could only be realized through the indirect assistance of the other hegemony in each case.

3. Kaplan, Robert D., *Warrior Politics: Why Leadership Demands a Pagan Ethos*, New York, 2002: Random House, xxii and 201. Boot, Max, *The Savage Wars of Peace: Small Wars and the Rise of American Power*, New York, 2002,: Basic, xx and 428 pp. Gowan, Peter, 'Empire as Superstructure', Oslo, 2004, *Security Dialogue*, PRIO, Vol. 35(2): 258-261.

4. A military attack on Iraq bolstered the U.S. thesis that in principle all rogue states would be ready to provide shelter to terrorists, and that the elimination of Saddam Hussein's regime will spread democracy to all the other Arab countries. In addition, Iraq's territory contained a huge amount of oil and gas, waiting to be tapped by U.S. energy companies. Yet another line of argumentation used by the U.S. maintained that a successful U.S. invasion would convince the Arab countries to give up their resistance to a U.S.-Israel-propagated solution to the conflict between Israel and the Palestinians. Viewed through the prism of these plausible-sounding reasons, the European argument that terrorists are criminals, and must be brought to justice after being apprehended, was bound to fail.

5. The German government referred to the reluctant German parliament. Peter Schmidt, a security analyst at the German Institute for International and Security Affairs in Berlin, said: "The Americans quite often show up in Europe and the President tells us, 'Look I'll

never get that through Congress.' Something similar is happening here." (Cooper, Helene, in *International Herald Tribune*, Europe, February 6, 2008).

Officially, US representatives pay tribute to the civil engagement of European armies but the statement that follows their tribute articulates a combination of Europe's civil power and the US army's firepower. For a long time, US generals did not realize that US soldiers have to master both to be really successful on the battlefield.

6. In his prelude to the party conference of the Communist Party of China, China's president and party leader Hu Jintao made a surprisingly reserved statement regarding the unsolved question of Taiwan. He stated that "China is willing to undertake every effort to look for peaceful reunification" (*Frankfurter Rundschau*, October 16, 2007). Taiwan's Kuomintang party achieved a crushing victory in the last parliamentary elections, providing relief to the Chinese government in Peking (*Frankfurter Rundschau*, January 14, 2008).

7. "The record U.S. trade deficit with China is feeding complaints in Congress that the country artificially keeps its currency cheap to give its exporters an advantage over U.S. competitors. Lawmakers have introduced half a dozen measures aimed at China, including proposals to apply sanctions unless China lets the Yuan appreciate by 10 percent." (Kevin Carmichael and Matthew Benjamin, 'Congress keeps eye on U.S.-China talks', *International Herald Tribune*, May 21, 2007).

8. "What the Pentagon's planners want is a military alliance of the kind the U.S. has with South Korea and Japan. The U.S. is looking ahead at the next 50 years. Japan is a declining power and Korea is an unpredictable one. Alone in Asia, India offers a prospect of a power whose rise can be harnessed in order to help the US deal with the strategic challenge of China". (Siddharth Vardarajan, 'America, India and Outsourcing Imperial Overreach', *The Hindu*, July 13, 2005).

9. Harish Khare in *The Hindu*, July 21, 2005.

10. Mahapatra, Rajesh, 'India-U.S. nuclear deal key to better ties', *BusinessWeek*/online, February 28, 2006.
    Bush calls upon the „global power" India to join efforts in spreading democracy (*swissinfo*, March 3, 2006).

11. *The Hindu*, 29 July 2005.

12. Müller, Oliver, *Der Tagesspiegel*, February 6, 2006.

13. Summarized conclusions of the three-part seminar organized by the *ICC* (*India International Center*) and the *Association of Retired Senior IPS Officers (ARSIPSO)*. The tentative conclusions reached at the two closed door meetings on 15 January and 1 April were placed before an open session of the joint seminar on 1August 2005.

14. „Everyone talks of the engines behind India's economic boom, its information technology and the services provided to Western companies. But these are just ‚camels' that hardly need any infrastructure. They do not need to keep enormous factories fed, nor do they need to handle any heavy goods. They're just right for India's infrastructural desert. The World Bank reckons that India would have to spend about 12.5% of its gross domestic product on infrastructure year after year in order to catch up with its rival China by the year 2015. This is four times more than what is actually being invested." (Petersen, Britta,

'Wüste für Investoren – Indiens Hightech-Erfolge täuschen: Die Industrie hat es schwer im Land', *Die Zeit*, May 16, 2007).

15. Even while standing firm by their respective partners, USA and Russia will use every opportunity to make the most of their much-wooed position. Hidden contacts between them could even be used to play the arch-enemies off against each other, weakening China and India all the more.

16. Nevertheless, any China-India partnership remains a hegemonic relationship as far as smaller countries, both in direct proximity to or further away from both, are concerned.

17. The discourse about the USA being an "informal hegemony" dwells on this problem and suggests that the US will deliberately restrict its power.

18. Manmohan Singh had commented, "Till yesterday, India was looked [upon] as a pariah in the nuclear order. Today, the country has a place in it and there has been a complete makeover of the world view about India." (Seema Guha, India will not lose its nuclear swaraj: Manmohan Singh, *DNA-Mumbai-Daily News&Anaysis WORLD*, December 18, 2006).

19. Prime Minister Manmohan Singh is apparently firmly convinced that India is "too economically weak" (Bharat Karnad, 'Does India really count?', *Deccan Chronicle*, 29 June 2005). Jairam Ramesh, Indian minister for commerce: "We are not in [the] race. They have already won the race". Ramesh also said that Indians have started admiring the Chinese (Somini Sengupta, 'Competition between China and India goes beyond borders', *New York Times,* November 20, 2006).

20. "…The Manmohan Singh establishment will need to address itself to the middle class sentimentality. The middle class in India remain wedded to the Nehruvian idea of total autonomy in the pursuit of science and technology. Credible and honest assurances would need to be given – and believed – that nothing has been said or done in Washington that would put a cap on India's autonomous quest. This middle class sentimentality is at the core of the vision of 'India is destined to be a great power' and this longing needs to be harnessed positively and constructively." (Harish Khare, 'Selling the United States of America in India', *The Hindu*, July 21, 2005).

21. "The Iranian project is not only vital for India's medium-term energy security, it is also the key which will help us unlock the potential of a pan-Asian energy grid involving Central Asia and China as well. U.S. opposition to the pipeline is not just because of its antipathy to the Islamic regime that is in power there. It is because Washington knows the involvement of Iran in this kind of project will undo the efforts it has made all these years to dominate the transit routes of Asian energy."(Siddharth Varadarajan, 'A farewell to the gas pipeline?', *The Hindu*, July 22, 2005).

22. In the meantime Russia has supplied uranium to the Tarapur nuclear plant, thereby provoking a massive American protest (*Express India*, 'Russia defends decision', March 17, 2006).

23. K. Subrahmanyam, notably, propagated a different course, namely a six-power relationship involving USA, EU, Russia, China, Japan and India. K. Subrahmanyam, 'Lessons from Dialogues with European Security Experts', *Berliner Studien zur Interna-*

tionalen Politik und Gesellschaft, edited by Voll, Klaus and Beierlein, Doreen, Berlin 2006, Vol. 3, *Rising India – Europe's Partner?* (313-321).

24. „The former US President Jimmy Carter made an unusually sharp attack on the outgoing Prime Minister. In a BBC interview, Carter said that Blair's ‚unswerving support' for the Iraq War was ‚a great tragedy for the world'. Responding to a question as to how he regarded Blair's behavior towards Bush, Carter replied: 'Detestable, submissive, blind, plainly servile.' In: *Gewalt überschattet Blairs Abschiedsbesuch im Irak* (Netzeitung.de, May 20 2007) (Story from BBC NEWS: http://news.bbc.co.uk/go/pr/fr/-/2/hi/americas/6672035.stm, Published: 2007/05/19 09:50:08 GMT).

25. Herfried Münkler, 'Im Kampf gegen die Unordnung. Was viele Europäer nicht verstehen: In Irak ging es für das Imperium USA selbst um die Befriedung einer Peripheriezone', *Frankfurter Rundschau*, 28 August 2003.

26. According to Condoleezza Rice, the Russian leadership regards US efforts to offer Ukraine and Georgia NATO membership as a zero sum game (*Die Zeit*, December 27, 2007).

27. Azerbaijan needs good political relations with Iran to have a short access to its separated province of Nakhchivan. The direct route would cross the hostile country of Armenia and another indirect route goes through Georgia and Turkey.

28. During the East-West conflict a Co-ordination Committee (COCOM) was set up for this purpose in Paris; it operated till 1995.

29. Startled to hear Kagan's opinion of the United States, the former US ambassador John Kornblum cried out, "But that's not America!" (*Die Zeit*, January 24, 2008).

30. The simplest instruments are CDOs. Several CDOs packed together are referred to as super CDOs or CDO^2, CDO^3. Taken out of the bank and stored in special companies, their name changes to "special investment vehicle" (SIV) Buchter, Heike, 'Kippen jetzt die Kreditversicherer?', *Die Zeit*, February 7, 2008).

31. Thanks to Bretton Woods, the USA has the right to run up unlimited debt in its own currency. No other member state of the Bretton Woods institutions enjoys the same privilege. The fact that countries "effectively 'checked out' of the Hotel Capital Mobility built by the global financial architect" reduced the IMF's influence but it did not in any way diminish the privileged status bestowed upon the US by the principles of Bretton Woods in 1944.

32. The largest state-owned investment funds (assets in billion US dollars) are: Abu Dhabi Investment Authority, United Arab Emirates, 875; Government Pension Fund, Norway, 380; Government Investment Corp., Singapore, 330; Saudi-Arab's central bank, 289; Fund for Future Generations, Kuwait, 213; China Investment Corporation, 200; Temasek, Singapore, 108 (*Tagesspiegel*, April 13, 2008).The largest investors are: pension funds, 21,6; investment funds, 19,3; insurances, 18,5; investors of oil dollars, 3,8; Asian central banks, 3,1; hedge funds, 1,5; private equity companies, 0,7 (*Frankfurter Allgemeine Zeitung*, October 11, 2007).

33. At a US Congressional Committee Hearing on 23.10.2008, Alan Greenspan declared: "I was wrong in assuming that organizations – particularly banks – can best protect their shareholders and their capital funds by virtue of their vested interest" (Andreas Oswald in *Tagesspiegel,* October 25, 2008). However, he did not mention the USA's globalization strategy.

34. Methodologically speaking, the state can be placed above, below, next to or at the center of a society. If the approach is from the general to the particular and strictly hierarchical in nature, then either society or the state would occupy the highest position, thereby determining to the fullest extent the category beneath it. In this case, the state for some would, for instance, merely be left to take on the rearguard action of a dynamically advancing society, whereas others may, on the contrary, even declare it to be the engine of overall social development. If the state were to be placed at the center of society around which all else revolved, it would be the sole driving force of the whole, made up of the state and its outward social emanations. The social realms revolving around it would at best be provided a minimum degree of autonomy. However, if society and the state were to be explored as two equal but distinct poles that exist side by side and partly overlap, their mutual dependence and impact would form the core of the analysis. The latter perspective finds its equivalent in the historical development of state and society.

35. On 30th October 2008, T-online borrowed an article from the Washington Post and entitled it: "US banks pay fat dividends thanks to state support". According to this article, the 33 banks that benefited from the government's bail-out package planned to pay dividends to the tune of around 7 billion dollars in that quarter alone. In the next few years, the total dividend paid out by the banks could amount to 3.3 billion dollars. Wealthy institutional shareholders would now also stand to benefit from these disbursements.

36. In the process of the self-preservation of societies, the unstable formless counterbalance, which the hegemonial formations build up as a result of their varying periods of birth and decay as well as the now regular nature of their opposition, is counterpoised by the institutionalized power of the state. Although, like all the other actors, the state too lacks an assured insight into the future, it can nevertheless forestall easily recognizable negative developments in good time. Prominent among the wide range of state interventions for the self-preservation of societies are the following which, irrespective of the delimitation of hitherto known spheres of circulation, continue to remain in existence:
- Support of emerging hegemonial formations against already established ones – constantly exploring the room for flexibility open to hegemonial formations and the limits thereof.
- The state's intervention as arbiter (with or without recourse to state monopoly on the legitimate use of force)
- Keeping the public sphere, and within it the field of discourse, open for activating and reactivating floating elements.

If, in the world of today, the formless counterbalance of hegemonial formations comes into being beyond hitherto known boundaries, be it on a global or regional scale, this shift certainly contributes to the weakening of the traditional nation state, though the necessity to contrast the spatially expanded formless counterbalance of these formations with the appropriate counterpart of the state – a counterpoise necessary for the continued existence of these formations – remains wholly unchanged.

37. The determination of Fair Value through International Financial Reporting Standards (IFRS) is by no means clear-cut. The IFRS cannot function without auxiliary solutions; they grant companies voting rights and discretionary powers. „The further away the select manifestation of Fair Value from the market price, the less transparent the chosen approach and the more entrenched the path to de-objectified accounting." Therefore, in his article in the *Frankfurter Allgemeine Zeitung* (FAZ), Prof. Karlheinz Küting, Director of the Institute for Accounting (IWP) at Saarbrücken pleads for a less significant role for theory in accounting than for „that which is implementable in practice or important in the first place" (kib in LexisNexis – Deutschland, Article no. 113890, dated 21.03.2007).

38. Pulling oneself out of crisis situations by the bootstraps has virtually become the hallmark of social development in the US. This is well illustrated by efforts to overcome the lethargy of the late 50s by concentrating on the conquest of near-Earth space under the John F. Kennedy administration, coming to terms with the trauma of the Vietnam War in the second half of the 70s, abandoning „Star Wars" during the Reagan Presidency at the end of the first half of the 80s and effecting the technological change under Clinton at the turn of the century.

39. Through government bonds the state finances that portion of its expenditure that exceeds its revenue from taxes and duties. In the process, the state also runs up debts on the same scale both with domestic and foreign buyers, over the period of validity of the bonds. In doing so it commits itself to repay its debts, together with the interest agreed upon, by or at the end of the term of validity.

40. The State Secretary in the Federal Ministry of Finance, Jörg Asmussen, the economic advisor to Chancellor Merkel, Jens Weidmann – both strong advocates and promoters of deregulation in previous years and trained by Prof. Axel Weber, currently President of the Bundesbank (German Federal Bank) and likewise a proponent of the neo-classical theory – are standing examples of the heavy bias in choosing personalities to overcome the current financial crisis they have themselves helped create. For them, the state is meant to exclusively serve the market, and they have obviously failed to bring into the focus of their vision the complex relationship between state and society, either before, during or after their academic studies in economics.

41. The boom in the US between 1925 and 1929, driven by the rising tide of innovations revolving around the automobile sector and electrical household gadgets (the automotive industry together with road construction, petrol stations, automobile workshops, installment loans, insurance, truck logistics etc.) was accompanied by the Federal Reserve's "cheap money" policy from 1927. This expansive money policy was an important factor for the increase in stock market speculation, particularly in the credit-financed purchase of bonds. When the Federal Reserve began to initiate countermeasures against this development at the end of 1928, speculation on the stock markets had gained such momentum that the shortage of credit on the market had no effect whatsoever.

15. Bibliography

Albert, Matthias, *Zur Politik der Weltgesellschaft*, Weilerswist, 2002.

Barber, Benjamin R., 'Imperialism or Interdependence?', *Security Dialogue*, PRIO 2004, Vol.35(2): 237-242, 2004 PRIO. 'Clarifying the System Concept by Means of Methodological Pluralism', Paper for the Panel 'ES Theory Debates' WISC Conference, Istanbul, August 2005.

Barnett, M., 'Power in International Politics'/M. Barnett, R. Duvall, *International Organization*, 59(1) Winter 2005: 39-75.

Boot, Max, *The Savage Wars of Peace: Small Wars and the Rise of American Power*, New York, 2002: Basic, xx and 428 pp.

Brooks, Th., 'Hegel's theory of international politics: a reply to Jaeger', *Review of International Studies*, 30(1), January 2004: 149-152.

Buzan, Barry, *From international to world society? English school theory and the social structure of globalisation*. Cambridge: Cambridge University Press, 2004. xviii, 294 p. (B-O 172).

Checkel, J.T., 'Social constructivism in global and European politics: a review essay', *Review of International Studies* 6(1) March 2004: 49-244.

Cox, Michael, 'Empire by Denial? Debating US Power', *Security Dialog*, PRIO 2004, Vol. 35(2), p. 230.

Ferguson, Niall, 'Hegemony or Empire?' *Foreign Affairs*, September/October 2003.

Goodenough, Patrick, *CNSNews.com International Editor*, September 12, 2005: 'India Wants Closer Ties With US – But Also With Iran'.

Gowan, Peter, 'Empire as Superstructure', Oslo, 2004, *Security Dialogue*, PRIO 2004, Vol.35(2): 258-261.

Haller, Gret, *Die Grenzen der Solidarität: Europa und die USA im Umgang mit Staat, Nation und Religion,* 2nd ed., Berlin 2002.

Hegel, Georg Wilhelm, Friedrich, *Phänomenologie des Geistes*, Frankfurt/Main, 1973.

Hildebrandt, Reinhard, *Kampf um Weltmacht – Berlin als Brennpunkt des Ost-West-Konflikts*, Opladen 1987

Hildebrandt, Reinhard, *Globalisation & An American Empire*, Paper for the IPCS (Institute for Peace and Conflict Studies), New Delhi 11 0029, India, August 2, 2005.

Hildebrandt, Reinhard, *Globalisation – Its Influence on State and Society*, New Delhi 2005.

Hildebrandt, Reinhard, 'India's Entry into the Concert of World Powers', *Berliner Studien zur Internationalen Politik und Gesellschaft*, edited by Voll, Klaus and Beierlein, Doreen, Berlin 2006, Vol. 3, Rising India – Europe's Partner? (212-221).

Ikenberry, John, 2001, 'American Power and the Empire of Capitalist Democracy', *Review of International Studies* 27: 191-212.

India International Centre (ICC) and the Association of Retired Senior IPS Officers (ARSIPSO), summarized conclusions of the three-part seminar held by India International Centre (ICC) and the Association of Retired Senior IPS Officers (ARSIPSO). The tentative conclusions reached at the two closed door meetings on 15th January and 1st April were placed before an open session of the joint seminar on 1st August 2005.

International relations theory, GNU Free Documentation, http//en.wikipedia.org/International relations theory.

IR Theory Web Site, Altavista, *Paradigms, Approaches and Theories*.

Jackson, R., *Classical and modern thought on international relations: from anarchy to cosmopolis*, New York, 2005.

James, P., 'Chinese choices: a poliheuristic analysis of foreign policy crisis', 1950-1996, *Foreign Policy Analysis*, 1(1) MARCH 2005, 31-54.

Kang, D.C., 'Hierarchy, balancing and empirical puzzles in Asian international relations', in: *International Security*, 28(3), Winter 2003-04: 165-180.

Kaplan, Robert D., *Warrior Politics: Why Leadership Demands a Pagan Ethos*, New York, 2002: Random House, xxii and 201.

Karnad, Bharat, 'Does India really count?', *Deccan Chronicle*, 29 June 2005.

Laclau, Ernesto/Mouffe, Chantal, *Hegemonie und radikale Demokratie*, Wien, 1991.

Luhmann, Niklas, Die Gesellschaft der Gesellschaft, Frankfurt am Main, 1997.

Majeski, S.J., 'Asymmetric power among agents and the generation and maintenance of cooperation in international relations', *International Studies Quarterly*, 48(2) June 2004: 455-470.

Mann, Michael, *Die ohnmächtige Supermacht – Warum die USA die Welt nicht regieren können*, Frankfurt/New York, 2003.

Mouffe, Chantal (ed.), *Dekonstruktion und Pragmatismus – Demokratie, Wahrheit und Vernunft*, Wien, 1999.

Münkler, Herfried, 'Im Kampf gegen die Unordnung. Was viele Europäer nicht verstehen: In Iraq ging es für das Imperium USA selbst um die Befriedung einer Peripheriezone', *Frankfurter Rundschau*, 28 August 2003.

Mustafa, Seema, 'The Nobodies', *The Asian Age*, 30 July 2005.

Nadkarni, J.G., 'Terms of India-U.S. Endearment', *The Asian Age*, 30 July 2005.

New York Times, September 24, 2006.

Nye, Jr., Joseph S., *The Paradox of American Power: Why the World's Only Superpower Can't Go It Alone* (New York: Oxford University Press, 2002), xviii + 222pp.)

Nye, Jr., Joseph S., 2003, 'American Power and Strategy', *Foreign Affairs* 83(2): 39-49.

Report on World Economic Forum, *domain-b.com*, September 26, 2006.

Rosen, Stephen Peter, 2003, 'An Empire, If You Can Keep It', *The National Interest* 71, Spring: 51-61.

Saull, Richard, On the ‚New' American ‚Empire', *Security Dialogue*, Vol. 35(2): 250-253.

Shell, Kurt L., *Bedrohung und Bewährung*, Westdeutscher Verlag, Berlin 1965, 36.

Subrahmanyam, K., 'Lessons from Dialogues with European Security Experts', *Berliner Studien zur Internationalen Politik und Gesellschaft*, edited by Voll, Klaus and Beierlein, Doreen, Berlin 2006,Vol. 3, *Rising India – Europe's Partner?*, 313-321.

Tellis, Ashley, *India as a New Global Power: An Action Agenda for the United States*, Carnegie Endowment for International Peace, 2005.

Tønnesson, Stein, 'The Imperial Temptation', *Security Dialogue* 2004 PRIO, Vol. 35(3): 329-343.

Underhill, Geoffrey R.D., *Global Financial Architecture, Legitimacy, and Representation: Voice for Emerging Markets*, Garnet Policy Brief, No. 3, January 2007.

Varadarajan, L., 'Constructivism, identity and neo-liberal (in) security', *Review of International Studies*, 30(3), July 2004: 485-498.

Varadarajan, Siddharth, *The Hindu*, July 29, 2005.

Varadarajan, Siddharth, A farewell to the gas pipeline? *The Hindu*, July 22, 2005.

Venugopal, K., *The Hindu*, July 22, 2005.

Voll, Klaus, 'Globale asiatische Großmacht? Indische Außen- und Sicherheitspolitik zwischen 2000 und 2005', *Berliner Studien zur Internationalen Politik und Gesellschaft* (edited by Klaus Voll and Uwe Skoda), Vol. 2, Berlin, 2005.

Voll, Klaus and Beierlein, Doreen, *Berliner Studien zur Internationalen Politik und Gesellschaft,* Berlin 2006, Vol. 3, Rising India – Europe's Partner?

Wade, Robert Hunter, 'Bringing the Economic Back', *Security Dialogue*, PRIO 2004, Vol. 35(2): 243-249.

Wallerstein, Immanuel, *The Modern World System: Capitalist Agriculture and the Origins of the European World Economy in the Sixteenth Century*, Academic Press, August 1997.

Wendt, Alexander, *Social Theory of International Politics*, Cambridge, 1998.